# The Dolphin's Arc

# The Dolphin's Arc

## Poems on
## Endangered Creatures of the Sea

Elisavietta Ritchie, Editor

with Illustrations by Julia S. Child

SCOP Publications, Inc.
College Park, Maryland

The Dolphin's Arc: Poems on Endangered Creatures of the Sea
Copyright ©1989 by SCOP Publications, Inc.
Editor: Elisavietta Ritchie

Special thanks for monetary, editorial, artistic, clerical, and moral support to:

David Doubilet, who contributed the cover photograph; Julia S. Child, who contributed
the illustrations; The Center for Marine Preservation (originally The Center for Environ-
mental Education), especially Armin Kuder, Roger McManus, Tom Grooms, Joseph
Stinson, Rose Bierce, Jill Perry, and Susan Christy for their encouragement; The D.C.
Commission for the Arts and Humanities, the late Jenny von Lerche Erhardt, and the
Norton and Nancy Dodge Foundation at Cremona, Maryland for financial backing;
Merrill Leffler, Lucia Dunham, Maxine Combs, Ann Darr, Hilary Tham, Juliana Field,
Sarah Cotterill, and Donna Wirth, who helped organize and proofread the manuscript;
SCOP editors Mary Swope, Stephanie Demma, Katharine Zadravec, and Stacy Tuthill;
Will Inman, Jean Voege, and Paula Bonnell and all the other poets who encouraged the
editor to persist with the project and donated their poems to it.

Since this page cannot legibly accommodate all copyright notices, pp. 163-165 constitute
an extension of the copyright page.

Library of Congress catalog number: 89-60251
ISBN No. 0-930526-11-2

SCOP TWELVE in a series
Printed in the United States of America
SCOP Publications, Inc.
Box 376, College Park, Maryland 20740

# TABLE OF CONTENTS

## I. CELEBRATION

## II. MAN & CREATURE

## III. SLAUGHTER

## IV. ELEGY

## V. REINCARNATION

# EDITOR'S NOTE

Poets are by nature, I think, environmentalists. As the poems in this collection suggest, we not only often draw inspiration from the natural world, but are deeply concerned about it. Environmentalists, working close to nature, fighting to preserve it, live amid the raw stuff of poetry.

I conceived of this anthology to reach both scientific and literary audiences. In particular, through the sale of the book I hope to raise needed funds for the Center for Marine Conservation — the umbrella organization for The Whale Protection Fund, The Seal and Sea Turtle Rescue Funds, and the Marine Habitat Program.

I sent out a call for poems on whales, dolphins, sea turtles, seals, and sea lions. Poems poured in from all regions of the country; some also celebrated walruses, sea elephants, sea cows — even one octopus. Everyone was enthusiastic about a project concerned with restoring the environment. Many good poems had to be returned for lack of space. It has taken several years to choose, arrange, edit, fund, and finally to publish *The Dolphin's Arc*, earlier called *Tide Turning*. As can be seen from the brief biographical notes, the 109-poem collection includes poets from 32 states and one from Chile. There was room only to suggest the wealth and variety of honors, credentials, and publications this gathering of American voices represents.

As if poetry could halt a slaughter. Like hurling a pebble at an armored tank. As Deena Metzger writes, "If it were only a question of whales." We face (or avoid) so many immense problems — the threat of nuclear war; actual wars forever breaking out somewhere on the globe; constant, universal dangers of pollution, hunger, homelessness, disease, overpopulation, man's inhumanity to man — and to animal. But the wanton killing of whales, the overdevelopment that deprives sea turtles of their birthing beaches, and the dolphins strangled in tuna nets — these are not simply metaphors for all the world's ills. They are problems in themselves. As American poets, we can focus attention on them, to help change the broad environmental policies of all the nations.

The French writer Albert Camus said, on accepting the Nobel Prize for Literature:

> Art is a means of moving the greatest number of people by offering them a privileged picture of common sufferings and joys. Art therefore obliges the artist not to isolate himself . . . The silence of an unknown prisoner, abandoned to humiliations at the other end of the earth, suffices to draw the writer out of his exile, each time, at least, that in the midst of the privileges of liberty, he manages not to forget this silence and to make it resound by means of his art.

The whales, dolphins and other sea creatures threatened with extinction, who seem so free, joyous, and self-contained, have become silent prisoners whom we must champion. The survival of the sea affects Earth's survival — and our own. For, as Richard Wilbur writes in the final poem of this collection:

> . . . What should we be without
> The dolphin's arc, the dove's return,
> These things in which we have seen ourselves and spoken?

— Elisavietta Ritchie
Washington, D.C.
December, 1988

This book is dedicated to my late parents
each born far from the sea
who gave me my love of oceans:
George Leonidovich Artamonoff,
born in Kursk, Russia,
and
Jessie Downing Artamonoff,
born in Kansas City, Missouri.

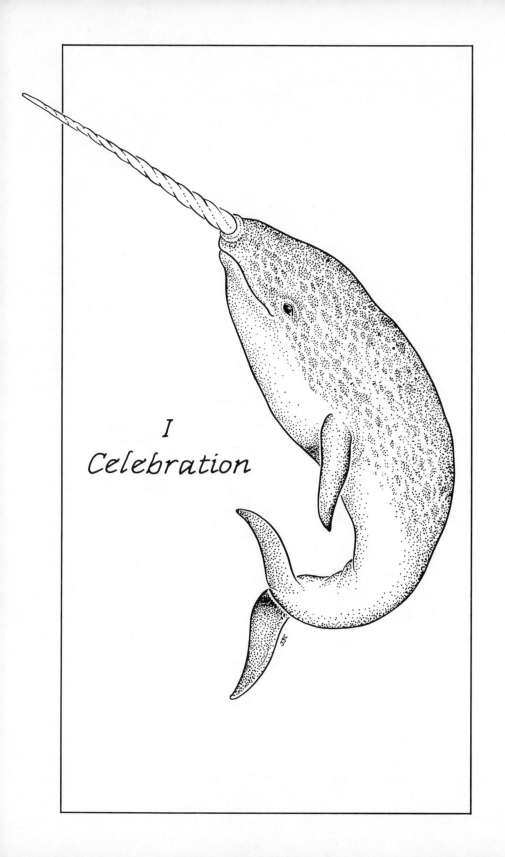

I
Celebration

*Constance Urdang*

## THE OTHER LIFE

I know in my other life I am a whale
Surfacing rarely, blunt as a club, singing
In my rusty cracked voice
Like the creaking timbers of a clipper ship
Persistent cantatas mixed with the thump and swish
Of enormous waves, the ground bass
Of the ocean; or silent
To hear the answering song of distant kin.
Profound and dark, my echoing apartments.
My element is salt, like tears.
I move in it alone, light as a shadow.
Beached, I grow monstrous, helpless, and grotesque.

*Roger Pfingston*

# THE NEWT AND THE WHALE

1.
Waiting to go
to the whale symposium
I turn the porch light on
and open the door to look out
but look down instead
to what seems at first
a twig or a blade of grass
wriggling to the beat of rain.

I go down on my knees
and the tiny black eyes
of a newt stare up,
holding me fast
before it streaks,
half swimming, propelled
by the swish of its tail
down a crack in the porch.

2.

After the symposium, right whales
swim and grunt in the ocean of my head.
Their breaching leaves me exhilarated,
envious. One swims up head-on,
looking like a submarine, and asks
for a poem. I don't know what to say.
He nuzzles my hand and I touch his eyebrow
that grows like a patch of lichen.
He swims away as if to give me time
to compose myself, then comes round again
darkening the water with his slow passing,
gently grazing my body with one fluke.
Heading out to sea, he picks up speed
and I seem to know that this one's for me
as he rises, pectoral fins waving wildly
as if to lift the scarred tonnage
out of a dazzle of sea-spray into flight
before he finally plunges back-first
with a deafening boom, smacking a hole
in the ocean the size of a freight train,
great walls of water roaring and folding in
above him until they crash and explode
in a crystalline shower unlike any
Roman fountain now or ever.
                              He swims back
and again asks for a poem. It's the least
I can do, thinking as I begin, *What luck*
*this night, the joy of the newt and the whale!*

# I ASK THE WHALE, WHY?

For my spout is seen for miles.
  It is the bright phallus
  women see through
  to their doom.
For an ancient, fabulous city
  thrives within me.
  You can visit it safely
  in your dreams
  and wake up smiling.
For my bulk is legendary.
  I have floated from the head of God.
  I mistake mountains for mates.
For my tail is a tower.
  When it falls, it does not
  tell children from murderers.
For I am sleek.
  The water finds its purpose
  in holding still
  as I pass through it.
For playing on my back in water
  I am the proof of miracles.
For my mouth is the slit
  God made to test creation.
For I follow you
  when you go inland.
  I circulate in your blood
  and you grow to accommodate me.

*Sheila Nickerson*

## WHALE

Pole to pole
I am geometry of roundness,
An unsharp algebra.
Only soft numbers fit
My sonic opera.
That is why you cannot
Understand, O man of angles.
We school in different shapes.
Between alpha and omega I swim.

The physics of completion.
Tide to tide, year to year,
I make the journey, round.
Equator is just a line
You put there since you
Must — you who think in halves,
Not wholes, in corners, not
In shapes of earth and sea,
Of igloos, moons, and me.

*James Bertolino*

## CONSIDER THE WHALES
*(an acrostic)*

Let's consider seven whales
easing onto a beach
torn by a storm into valleys and
small mounds of shell and weed

marvel for a moment how their breathing
ascends the wind, notice pasty
krill along their mouth parts, their
even-tempered gaze

lie down then alongside one in the sand, bare leg
over tail fin, and begin to listen . . .
very soon the song of the galaxy invades
each pore and ear of your unfolding

*Brewster Ghiselin*

## ORCA

Beastblack under a fin torpedo-swift
In a glaze of sun offshore that is torn with motion
Whales like gods of the dolphins flip and fall
And pour the lift of their dives like the surf's backs.

Slant of their fins asway like a wing speeding
And heads rising blunt like a feeding swallow's
They circle, black and white in their green foam,
With ease of swallows over the water, in air.

What they are feeding on we believe we know.

These are the steep rocks, white with guano
Over the deep seethe and list of the ocean,
That always re-echo the bark and bawl of sea lions.
A long while after the sheet of the sea is smooth
Only the gulls and the cormorants over their shadows
Will cross the light. And the brown rocks will cry.

*Frederick Morgan*

## WHALE POEM

All of the bones of five toes are in each of his paddles
and under the blubber the bones of unused hind legs.

The tail (unlike a fish's, horizontal)
is rudder and propeller both, and drives him
with strength of seventy horses abruptly down
hundreds of feet to depths at which his body
must bear many tons of pressure per square inch.

Rising, he may release the used-up breath
just before reaching the surface: at such times
a mixture of water and breath blows up from the sea.

I read about him first in Kipling's story — how
the sailor he swallowed foxed him by blocking his throat —
but the truth about the baleen whale was more surprising.
His mouth is a maze. He has no teeth.
Enormous plates of horn in the upper jaw,
frayed at the edges as though rough-combed for use,
lie flat, toward the throat, when the mouth is closed —
when it opens, they are raised and hang down like fringed curtains.
As he swims through the sea pen-mouthed, a living cavern,
thousands of little life-forms are trapped in the fringes;
when the mouth closes, the water strains out at the sides
but these remain and fall down on the tongue to be swallowed.
(They have to be small — his throat couldn't take in a herring!)

A sperm whale, on the other hand, can swallow a Jonah
or something still larger. His mouth takes up one third
the length of a body that may extend sixty feet.
The sperm oil lies in a cavity alongside his head
and ambergris — used as fixative in making perfumes —
may, when he's in poor health, form in his guts.
It used to be found in great masses, floating on southern seas.

The whale I saw in '49 or '50
was a smaller kind, maybe a grampus — I'd say
about twenty-five feet. He surfaced off our boat
(Eddie Sherman's lobster-boat, which Dr. Moorhead
had chartered for his annual fishing trip:
we had our lines out, anchored in the mouth of Blue Hill Bay)
one hundred yards out to sea, and blew and spouted —
a hollow whistling more vibration than sound —
then sank, and surfaced once more about ten minutes later
on our other side, a little bit closer — and we laughed.
We got the message: greatness, freedom, and ease.

They're mammals; the mothers nurse their young.
We hunt them, sink our barbs into their flesh —
using explosives now in our harpoons —
hoist the vast bleeding bodies to the decks
of "factory ships," where the live flesh is rent from the bone.
They may have thoughts in their heads: we do not know.

Sometimes I think of the great sum of pain
endured by inoffensive giant bodies
torn, ripped, chopped, dismembered in their millions
by the sharp tricks of a smart race of maggots.
Is there justice in the universe? We'd better hope not.

I had a dream once, in which I was swallowed by a whale
and thought it was the end and something horrible —
but it all opened up, like the Mammoth Cave,
in long strange hallways — stalactites, stalagmites gleaming —
and light in the distance where someone was waiting for me.

They may have thoughts — we do not know. But far
beneath the surface, where a few still live and play,
they summon each other in high-pitched signalings
and sing deep day-long songs we'll never learn.

## CETUS, A LETTER FROM JONAH

The whales
are singing.
They answer
each other.
They move
through the water
repeating
strange verses.
Listen, God.
Listen.

I would be frightened
if it were not
for the singing.
I move through a space
where Cetus,
at midnight,
is swimming
toward
Delphinus
singing.

## LEVIATHAN

Morning touches the waves and breaks
      over the whitecaps where the ship cuts
through the waters turning an early blue.
      The wind is fresh in the east.
Spume rinses the deck now and again;

      the light strengthens, the sun riding
      a high scud in rising flight.
Nothing is to the horizon beyond
      susurruses of the sea.
The ship rolls, and as she rolls she waits.

      Then sunlight touches a fountain
      rising from ocean abeam.
The ship shudders into pursuit at flank.
      A sharp sound shatters the wind.
A coil of line unwinds, following

      its shaft over the combers. Stain
      tints the fluid of a wave,
and a great fluke rises into the air,
      then falls in an explosion
of froth as the leviathan sounds.

      Beneath it the waters glitter;
      with depth, they begin to dim.
Before it, in the fathoms, there is night
      perpetual and cold; there
is darkness rising breathless and deep.

*Sarah Brown Weitzman*

## WHALES TO OCEANUS

they went forward
finally to fathoming
their former life

refusing to walk
earth gracelessly
but eased in water

they drew up their feet
to mime the freedom
of fins, yet kept

their milk and bursting
breath and blood
like ours, animals

still that left
land and the stolid
solid life behind

*Hillel Schwartz*

# ON THE WHALES OF THE CALIFORNIA DESERT

They were there once,
immense tumbleweeds
floating in the hot air,
light as myth,
grazing above the scrub oak,
the monkey flower,
mountain mahogany.
Lizards would follow
their shadows and mark
the paths of their flight.
Sometimes, settling
into the sand, the whales
would leave soft impressions
visible centuries after.
These are what we look for,
and bones caught in the wild lilac.
When the floods came
the whales moved out into the sea
and learned their mass.
But there are moments,
turning inland, when they come up,
sensing the cactus.
This is why they breed
so close to our shore.
This is why, from time to time,
some strand themselves on our beaches,
struggling to fly
back to their desert.

*Robert Siegel*

# THE GREAT WING OF NEW ENGLAND
## *(Megaptera Novaangliae)*

From sounding the depths off Martha's Vineyard
you rise, a sudden black mountain
through the sea's green flanks marbled with white
and beat the air with ghostly wings,
crashing on your back, spouting your music,
your eye wrinkled and wise, humorous by your flipper.

Through miles of krill, taking vast harvest
or idling, you roll in a radiance, waiting
for the nightly rush of love toward Orion,
for your mate who floods the sea with her milk
in the moon's dairy while the mouth of her calf
drinks and churns the stars floating above him.

I hear your song where I lie listening
to the waves of grass in an ocean of land —
your croon, your whistle like birds skipping
on a barnacled back or water dancing,
your echo searching a thousand sea-canyons,
your groan like the ice at the end of the world.

*Kathryn Nocerino*

## NARWHALS

---

   under the water
  they click their horns together —
horns spiraled, straight,
 as tall as flagpoles
(sold in ancient times as unicorn,
  ground into aphrodisiacs).
 the clicks, under the surface of the water,
  sound like thuds:
surreal combat on a private stage —
 Douglas Fairbanks and the Black Knight,
  both armed from the forehead.


   sometimes narwhals,
    dead or ailing,
  limping into hospital,
   have lengths of horn imbedded in their sides —
the evidence of war, perhaps;
   or love.

## WHALE TIME

Whales at play
Take their time,
Their time being as long as they.
One whale kisses a fin
With saline pungency.
An hour later
She kisses the spout.
Her lover says,
"Not so fast,
Let us love at leisure,
My sweet whale woman."

*Barbara A. Holland*

## HARBOR SEALS

First one, then two,
another some distance off,
break through the satin
of the water about the boat.

Those harbor seals
like elderly gentlemen
at the club,
their whiskers quivering
to know what these oars are doing.

*John Tagliabue*

## SMOOTH AND GLEAMING

Spending the day
    looking at seals,
    slippery subject, dousing the whiskers,
whistling at the wind and the svelte of wetness, belly and
    belief, nose
diving and tail flipping, figuring with water as
    Taoism does. Estuary
somewhere off Eden or South Harpswell. Once I was a
    loon there. Now 5 seals.
The silver light of the flickering water is active
    with everywhere motion.
The sports of slipperiness snort in a presence
    beyond applause.

*Paula Bonnell*

## THEY ARE RIGHT; THEY ARE AWARE; THEIR AWARENESS IS RIGHTNESS, BUT THEY ARE NOT AWARE OF THAT

Fine animals are full of certainties —
the seals seen from a glass tunnel underwater
rise like balloons to break the surface.
They refill themselves with air
and plunge like whales diving for sanctuaries
which they themselves contain
oxygen deep below the thermocline.

Such certainties pause as well as move —
the cat immediate before prey
is a conjunction of attention and intention
made salient with shivers of its fur.
This cat could pause as long as burros
who await Godot
after Vladimir and Estragon have left
and even after Ferlinghetti has gone.

And now while cat, burros, clowns and poet
jubilantly cross the border of this verse,
the seals and whales ascend
to bark brown zoos into spring
and breach with plumes in arctic whitenesses
under effulgent skies.

A. Poulin Jr.

# CHILDREN IN FOG

*To Michael Waters*

Ebbtide: a thin fog sails in from the sea
and moors on the Atlantic
coast. Houses vanish, our neighbors on
the beach start to dissolve

and each thin strand of hair on our bodies
turns to white, heavy with
a warm and gentle sea-mist. Suddenly,
we are figures in this land-

scape's dream again, floating in and out
of one another with the heave
of tides and exchanging histories
like breath in lover's mouths.

In our children's eyes, we are fathers
flying toward the vanished point
of their own history, returning only
in their dreams, as we always

will; and where the sea and the horizon
fuse, they are baby dolphins
leaping out of breakers, stuttering that
music we inhaled, once, long

ago and hammered into tongues of law.
Neither males nor females of
their species, they still love themselves so much
they are buoyant in this mist,

their wake bright parabolas of light. They swim
toward us so slowly; they could
never reach us in our lifetime or their own.
Michael, they are so substance-

less, they might also dive into our eyes
and nest there deep inside
our brains to resurrect as memories
remembered in another life.

The landscape dreams us into motion;
we dream ourselves leaping from
a brilliant sea; we wake in
an imaginary country,

strangers in these strangers' heavy bodies
white with frost, a music in
our throats as intricate as scrimshaw
replicas of our descendants —

and we drown, only to awaken once
again, here, on the Atlantic
coast, as our children's names soar from our open
mouths until they swim toward us

again and we know they are still safe.
In this haze that has become
as much light as it is water, Michael,
this could be the day when

children of the sea first breathed oxygen
and miraculously walked
on land — or that other, when the offspring
of this earth long for hydrogen

again, unleash its law that will impose
a momentary order
all its own, when, like the other fathers,
we'll come to this coast again

and wait for our bodies' every sinew
to blaze brightly, from within,
for our children's bodies to collapse
around their feet like starfish,

while the music from their vanished mouths
will leap back into the breakers,
back into the throats of dolphins swimming,
slowly swimming in our eyes.

*David B. de Leeuw & Madeline Tiger*

## THE PASSING OF DOLPHINS

    bluegreen bodies
    moving sleekly in the ocean

in an undulance of
thick waters they
glide forward, dart,
leap and dive and
rise
in a rhythm like
breathing bodies
belling and sighing
they surge

    sometimes in a distant
    glimmer high enough
    to clarify
    the difference between
    swimmer and water
    or in the unintentional
    celebration of
    movement and the embodiment
    of movement, rising in light
    and falling or
    diving
    to carry that light
    to its limits of
    darkness, the dolphin goes
    down in the unfathomable
    ocean, the ocean
    receiving the swimmer
    becoming part of
    the perpetual journeying,
    parting as it is forced
    to part for the undesigned
    passage of the dolphins,
    who manage by ignorant swerve
    and arc, without plot
    or meditative power, to go
    forward, warm in the deep
    cold, unrewardable and continuous

their motion suddenly merging
mammal and element, now
indistinguishable although not
forever to keep this obscure
unity: only in the most intense
passages the waves
thicken, becoming
the backs of the dolphins,
palpable as flesh which
in its rising and returning
seems to turn into
water but passes and darts forward
in its own embodiment
of line, skin, density, muscle, eye,
flipper, tail, air; specific
in its motion
in its element

*Brian Swann*

## PIG MOON, TURTLE MOON

The moon's horns stick
into sky's wall.
Shine like a tusk.
Pig moon. Moon
of the feral sow farrowing
on beds of last year's leaves.
She nuzzles her newborn
as they struggle
in the brief let-down
for the richest teats,
for milk rich as the sea.
The crack of waves
makes her stare toward
the beach. For this is also
the moon of the turtle eggs.
Moon of the loggerhead who has
paused just above the silt-weighted waves
to smell the air.
Leaving a tank track,
she drags her carapace past
waiting ghost crabs into low dunes.
She chooses her spot, scoops
out a pocket with front flippers.
Settles herself. Goes into
her egg-laying trance.
Soon, first one, then many
white globes with the fresh
shadow of centuries upon them
drop from her.
She will pull back the sand,
tamp it, tired; scatter her traces.
Down in the dark,
the germs of life will float
to the top of their yolks,
hang over their yellow ocean,
black moons clamped onto their sky's shell,
waiting for their tide.

*Julia Older*

## CARETTA CARETTA

The loggerhead turtle
swims slowly toward the dunes
where she deposits a hundred
moons wet and white as porcelain
in a black hole.

Raccoon eclipse
who would steal night
scampers across the sand
and bolts down all but one
that hangs luminous and fragile
in a far corner of Cassiopeia.

*Fredda S. Pearlson*

## NIGHT WATCHING
### (Jupiter Island Sounds)

*In the summer, giant turtles (leatherback, loggerhead and green) return to their birthplace to give birth to their young. Less than one percent of the hatchlings survive to maturity.*

Only now does she emerge
from some quiet wave, impossible
to see but for the moonlight
on her wet scarred back.
Hours on the dry summer sand
and the heat, the digging
in darkness, the effort of eggs
those large pearls she has brought
to shore. Finally
rushing out of her, the eggs
are perfectly round
thin as light.

Dozens and dozens of eggs now
needing only time
and the warmth of sand.
She covers them unaware
that she is being watched.
Soon the raccoon will have
his next unprotected meal.
Soon the men will sell the eggs
on the mainland, whispering
the promise of an aphrodisiac.

She crawls back to the sound of home
pushing the sand slowly behind her.
With the next wave even her tracks
will be gone.
In the middle of the next moon
the remaining ones will unfold
like so many dark gloves
reaching to find
the snapping white foam
in the moonlight.

*Arthur McA. Miller*

## SONGS FOR THE SEACOW

### 1. Becalmed (c. 1756)

It was seventeen days with no
water laid like flatiron on the sail.
No wrinkle of air on water;
our scuppers opened like elbows.

Then feet got narrow, yellow, like rough boards
on deck. Our hands cracked old rope
sideways in cleats. Nothing
but rum, no water; amber sloshes in the cup.

Seventeen days we lolled in the sail's shade,
prayed for a flush of gulls
from the long green line of land.

Water broke from her shoulders, then,
out near the green, her cheeks were full fat sunrise
soft as wind; the bounty, Lord, of her body

flushed with water, and nipples
washed in the sea . . . Her eyes flashed out
the color of rum soaked into mine forever.

### 2. (c. 1974)

In the tidal river
she floats like a bladder of muscle;
if you could see
down through the green, solid
like a TV screen gone all one color,
you'd catch her grazing upside down
below the hyacinths, as if a clever pig
inverted, were to graze off heaven.
Her muzzle wallows pulpy bulbs;
it sorts them out. Green mush
turns yellow in her teeth.
Seen from above, a patch of flowers
humps over, then sucks down.
The water furls her bulk; her hind feet
flip the surface phosphate green.

*Beth Joselow*

## WALRUS FACTORY

In the walrus factory: Attention
To tusks, attention to coarse follicles,
Whiskers short, black, blue mist of nostrils, lung
Power, stretched tension of tough hide, wrinkled,
Correct proportion of dewlap to throat.

Cuspids, bicuspids, molars, a brown mourn of
Tiny face over mountainous hard packed
Muscle, with plenty of fat, ears punched through
Skullbone, a mouth as round as a sea stone,
A voice that drowns even its own music.

Fins without slap, dull nails and obvious
Problems of assembly, the quirks of craft,
As despite a modern working method
The brown glass eyes glisten, vulnerable
And moist the moment they are inserted.

II
Man & Creature

*Ernest Kroll*

## MAMMALS

The sailor, shipwrecked, treading
The prayer wheel of water, who's
Suddenly buoyed up solidly
Forward into walkable
Shallows
      can thank a dolphin's
Whelping for his own helping with a
Lift.
   The plankless sailor, limbs
Thrashing to keep a deck on the
Deep —
      so like her own fresh-born
Helpless whelp into the sea
Expelled without a shift to
Stave off death, alone —
             can bank
Upon a dolphin's memory to quick
Latch *on:*
      mammals, drowning, must
Catch a lift to draw a breath.

## SEALS

For months desperate for lemons and a passage
the Russian ship noses through the fog
into yet another glacial amphitheater,
                                        the butt of a continent.
            Then a richness of seals
                        swims out of the deep to admire them,
                    philosophers blinking in leather caps.
Because they look like men or perhaps women
                    the sailors wave them aboard,
                offer them the bridal suite.
            Under the ship's swaying lamp they play cards for days,
but they don't speak or eat their precious bread,
                    smacking their lips, satisfied with their own oil.
And so they reverse engines,
                        go speeding back across the tropical seas,
                zealous teenagers breaking out in pustules
                past the native women waving from the tops of palms
to spend a day cashing in their mothers' inheritances
                in the gilded halls of St. Petersburg.
They return with the speed of the famished,
                with new knives carve their initials,
                    those of their girlfriends from tree to tree,
build churches, onions they leave behind that glow from within,
                beacons for their families, here, there along the coastline,
while by now having forgotten how to swim,
                        like actors losing their lines on stage,
                the seals have walked out embarrassed on their flippers.
They pick up the bright axes they find
                for centuries waiting for them far inland,
                    the boots they put on, the woolen caps
            that begin to fit, that go so well
with their moustaches as they begin to speak a husky French
                        better and better clearing a path faster each day.
            When they break through to the plains the Sioux
                don't know what to do with them, while behind
                        their daughters, educated at Bryn Mawr, Smith,
                squirm in paroxysm, fall to their knees, start barking.

*Daniel Hoffman*

## THE SEALS IN PENOBSCOT BAY

hadn't heard of the atom bomb,
so I shouted a warning to them.

Our destroyer (on trial run) slid by
the rocks where they gamboled and played;

they must have misunderstood,
or perhaps not one of them heard

me over the engines and tides.
As I watched them over our wake

I saw their sleek skins in the sun
ripple, light-flecked, on the rock,

plunge, bubbling, into the brine,
and couple & laugh in the troughs

between the waves' whitecaps and froth.
Then the males clambered clumsily up

and lustily crowed like seacocks,
sure that their prowess held thrall

all the sharks, other seals, and seagulls.
And daintily flipped the females,

seawenches with musical tails;
each looked at the Atlantic as

though it were her looking-glass.
If my warning had ever been heard

it was sound none would now ever heed.
And I, while I watched those far seals,

tasted honey that buzzed in my ears
and saw, out to windward, the sails

of an obsolete ship with banked oars
that swept like two combs through the spray

And I wished for a vacuum of wax
to ward away all those strange sounds,

yet I envied the sweet agony
of him who was tied to the mast,

when the boom, when the boom, when the boom
of guns punched dark holes in the sky.

*Brendan Galvin*

## SEALS IN THE INNER HARBOR

Ducks, at first, except they didn't
fly when we rounded the jetty
and swung into the channel,
didn't spread panic among themselves,
peeling the whole flock off the water,
but followed, popping under
and poking up as if to study our faces
for someone, their eyes rounded still
by the first spearing shock of ice,
or amazed to find our white town
here again, backed by a steeple
telling the hours in sea time.
Their skeptical brows seemed from a day
when men said a green Christmas
would fill this harbor with dead
by February. We left them hanging
astern at world's edge, afloat on
summer's afterlife: grey jetty,
water and sky, the one gray vertical
of smoke rising straight from a chimney
across the cove. We could believe
they were men who had dragged
this bottom till its shells were smooth
and round as gift shop wampum,
who never tied up and walked away
a final time, but returned for evenings
like this was going to be, thirsting
for something to fight salt off with,
needing a place to spit and plan
the rescue of children's children.

*Sarah Cotterill*

## HARP SEALS

1.
the cow nudges her young
between ice floes

dark-furred head a wedge
distinct above gray shuddering surface;

a just visible tremor passes down the length of her body
disappearing into water, as if a shock;
electricity coming to ground

as she faces sideways, one eye on the calves
one on the camera,
the hunter holding it

2.
we say we kill them for their fur
but it's really their voice we want
and the crescent
moon on their back

if only we could wear their skins a little while
maybe we could be
like them

feeling the wind as caress
ground as clear place with hollows
in the shape of our bodies

intimate with north
and true north

musicians at last for our own pleasure, and
hilarious, in spite of the hunter.

*Maxine Combs*

## FEBRUARY 11, 1983

Outside it's snowing hard enough to freeze a mammoth
which reminds me that traders near the Bering Sea
include in their vocabulary

a word that means to die of cold.
They also have a word
that means to die of longing.

Those Northern people knew a thing or two
about the gravities that down the heart;
they had the time to think them through

as they waited days to sight a seal's head
        in sea ice
or sat out winter nights in snow houses,
months away from a different season
        and the opposite of cold.

## AT LAND'S END

*"To grope down into the bottom of the sea . . . to have one's hands among the unspeakable foundations, ribs, and very pelvis of the world . . . "*
— Herman Melville, *Moby Dick*

Vertebrates,
we balance the skullcase of ancient apes
on centuries of discs slipped into place.
Flexed tissue tightening into muscle.

Cro-Magnons. Neanderthals. Homo Sapiens.
Brandishing bigger & better tools.
Lording it over our ancestors.

Believers in the burning bush.
Descendants of the tapped rock
from which our God springs. Ritual books
that gave us birthright over warmbloods
of sea air & field. Killing & taming.

All earth's creatures named,
nicks in the stock
of a thousand narrow tongues.

Specimens in drawers pinned to green velvet.
Bottles of formaldehyde. Pickled fetus bodies.
Toddlers tossing popcorn to curiosities
caged behind bars.

All those species relegated to the lower rungs
on the spiraling staircase of DNA.
All those we ignore.

All our relations.

But whales are different.
We do wonder about them,
their brains larger than ours.

Nursing one another in sickness. Singing
across bays. Leaping in the open air
for the sheer joy of leaping.

Risk aside, it is possible for us
to live hang-gliding on a wing of air.

But submerged underwater
we may as well be on the moon.

We move slowly. Our masks on.
Breath strapped to our backs.

*Nathaniel Tarn*

## JOURNAL OF THE LAGUNA DE SAN IGNACIO

Earth & upper air at peace. Sea still, air still. Still swift wings of the wind, still wave-lips. River mouths, torrents, springs, fountains: still. Silence, caverns of the universe. Again light, again dawn, again day, after the wandering dark.

> Immense architecture
> building in air
> towers and palaces
> from which their eyes look out
> like those of star denizens
> living in the heights
> as they live below,
> building in air
> and undersea
> their passage thru our life —
>     a gentle glide
> like a dream
> because no thing men know
> so huge and gentle at once
> can be other than dream
>     in such a world.
> Whales breathing
> all around us in the night
> just beyond the lights,
> seagulls like ghosts
> following the ship
> which seems to breathe
> yet never moves
> against the great Pacific's
> unfathomable shoulders

*

> The mountains rise out of the desert
> way out over Baja
> the whales rise out of the sea
> the mountains rise out of the sea
> the whales rise out of the desert
> the whales are taller than the mountains.

*

There was a man one time
got buried in a whale they say,
found bed and board down there
also some breakfast
found desk and library
and was granted extra knowledge
    (the whale a shaman they say).
          Cast from the human city,
he went down to the sea in whales
clothed with all his grave clothes
collected over the years
complete with turquoise necklace
and jadeite necklace
and one bead of jade —
his body full of sweet winds,
    he lay inside the whale
and wrote, in his death, terrible hymns
which no amount of pain
had ever torn from him
wrenched from his mouth
out thru his teeth
        in his mind's hearing . . .

*

Touching the skin of water
as it glides against water
slow slip of time
the black flesh gleaming like a hull
    (they call it Grey)
mottled with barnacles,
the imaginary touch
which men could have touched for centuries
    (instead of the carnage)
as it took them so long
to come to the beaches
to come to the sea
to come to the mountains

*

*D. E. Steward*

## PASSAGE

Approaching the Walvis Ridge and the tropic
Bearing for the Cape from night bunkering at São Vicente
Latitude 18.10 South, Longitude 3.52 East
Twelve thousand ton bulk carrier, cargo: Canadian wheat

For two full days and the morning of the next
Whales were everywhere around the ship
Good weather, calm seas
Mild-October and so spring on the African coast

Some sperms were first, it was 1963
Just south in the dry ocean off the desert
The baleen migration at full swell
Slicks of plankton surging in the sun

We steered our course at fifteen knots
Through herds, past solitary cows with calves
The horizon rising on their spouts
We felt joy, spirits lifted on the rail

Once a finback sounded portside
Came up on the starboard beam
And from the wing of the bridge
I looked it in the eye, could feel its breath

A hundred and thirty odd I counted
Until a day before landfall
We were past them all
They were gone, they are gone

*Michael Shorb*

## WHALE WALKER'S MORNING

Few records survive of the whale walkers
Of the 19th Century. Primarily American,
With a scattering of Dutch, Greek,
And African, the whale walkers
Based around the Boston-Nantucket area
Once numbered in the hundreds.

It has been said they counted both the Joseph's coat,
The Minoan seed pearl and the harmonica
Of the Indo-European Virgin among their lineage;
And that, unlike their leaner-visaged brothers
Of the harpoon, they staked their eliteness
To light around the feet, an ear tuned
To a keening wind, a finer sense of balance.

Of their concrete origins in sea crossings,
Tribal dances and the strut of mountain axemen
Not much more is known. Some have linked them
To rites among the Phoenicians,
To gypsies of the Asian Steppes,
To the tree at the edge of the world in Nordic mythology,
To intimates of the migration routes
And open country roads of the earth.

A few famous individuals, such as Nordo
The Aborigine, Jack Clappe, and Beartrap
Eddie, followed the practice of having
Their first whale tattooed on their chest.

The necessity of timing
The whale walking sessions
To coincide with the period
Just after early feedings
Along migration routes
Coupled with the necessity
For near perfect weather conditions
Led to the adoption of the popular
Turn-of-the-century phrase:
"It's a whale walker's morning," or, variously,
"A whale walker's morning to you and yours."

*James Ragan*

## BACKWARD YEARS

I.
These are backward years.
Dogs are not always dogs
or what they seem
to drunks or graveyard walls
who, merged in sleep, pose for leaks
or slow whimpers of midnight's passed wind.
Dogs, like grave diggers, hunt bones for reunions.

And whales are not always whales
or what they seem
to fish or fishermen,
who riding the tooth of a Jonah jaw
are spewed aground
like hunks of meat, beached rot-backs,
spawning worms with instinct.
Whales, like worms, control the spot they breed.

II.
We over-estimate our powers
of memory, the mind's dark tree,
hatchet, wind, stump, the swift slice
of a brain cut to size.
We leave such little proof of ourselves.

Unless by taming dogs
or whales, sonars of intelligence,
we can teach the weight of rumps and knees
and riders,
cocked like triggers, teaching death.

We thrive on amnesia —
forgetting men, like presidents and kings,
are only men
no matter what they seem
to all themselves or privately.
Even gods lose their minds
like children's toys
and are misplaced as simply
and as often
as they seem to matter.

*David Ray*

# THE HUMPBACKS

We know the humpback sings,
winters in Hawaii,
summers Alaska where
churning cruiseships make him
rage, flail the waters till
the tourists at the rail
think they understand him.
And yet they stay and stay,
recross again his bay
twelve glacial rivers feed.
A mother swims with dolphins
and Nikons capture them.
Above, a bald eagle
makes it all official:
this bay's an outdoor zoo
and voyeurs roam its paths.
At play whales flip icebergs,
a splendid show for noon.
And then they feed on shrimp,
two million at a scoop.
O wonderful splashers,
water-lashers, owners
of fins and flukes, baleen
once used for strong corsets
that bound our fat beauties,
let's see your triple ways
of feeding, tail that flicks
the chowder overhead —
wild net of bubbly spume,
fast-swimming till the shrimp
are centered for the grab
with one upward leap, stitch
of Great-gramma's needle
through the center of her hoop.
Your great jaws when skyward
resemble thick hands raised
in prayer — but that's absurd!
Or so the doubtful say.
And yet we hear a hymn
flung out toward distant stars,
wild creatures singing of

their love for waters we
assault with poisons, fill
with woe. Endangered whales,
White Eyes, Leviathan,
your absence will be part
of the long silence soon.

*Judith Hemschemeyer*

## DÜRER WENT TO SKETCH THE WHALE

Even though he could do marvelous rabbits
And had just won the patronage of Kaiser Karl,
Even though he had to travel by land
And by sea from Antwerp to Zealand,
Where it had been washed up dead on the shore,

Dürer went to sketch the whale. Because strange things,
*Seltsame Dinge*, interested him,
*Er wollte also den Wal skizzieren.*

And even though he arrived too late,
The whale having been washed back out to sea,
Even though he landed in a storm,
Fell into the harbor and almost drowned,
Contracting a strange, nearly fatal fever
*"Eine wunderliche Krankheit . . . "*
From which he suffered the rest of his life,

He had gone to sketch the whale. He went home
To Nürnberg then, with his wife, her servant,
All their baggage, his beloved Bible,
His collection of *seltsamen Dingen*
(Bits of coral, buffalo horns and so on)

And that most wonderful of all strange things,
His own calm, steady vision of this life
And the life to come: strong as the thrum of blood
Through the huge heart of a whale, minutely detailed
As its network of arteries and veins,
Pure, copious as its oil, *geballt*, rich
And solidly animal as chunks of ambergris.

*Joseph Bruchac*

# A SONG FOR OSEI BONSU

1.
In the cave cut by waves
deep into the red cliff
below the Fanti fishing village,
the Gulf of Guinea rushes in,
leaves lacy foam at the edge of sand
clean and white as cloud
where rests a single bone,
the height of a man.

It is the shrine of Osei Bonsu —
Chief Whale, Ghanaian people say.
They know the ocean
is not their own and, long ago,
took up that bone washed to their shores.
With chants and drumming,
they brought it here, a sign
from one who knows greater depths than theirs.

2.
The songs the Fanti people sing
when in their small boats far from land
are those learned from the calls of whales,
music heard late at night, remembered in dreams
when Chief Whale is a friend, a guardian.

3.
There are no shrines for any whale
here in my practical, western land.
That great rib bone which was left one night
by the storm which swept the beach at Keta
remains in Africa, though I carried it
back to the school where I then taught,
feeling for many days the thrill
of the power arced into that shape.

Yet, in this song, I return again
to that cave where some learn to recognize
a kinship of spirit which goes beyond
the shores where most visions end.

*Ann Darr*

## "HIT IT WITH THE BABY"

Rounding a corner in an open ocean
is quite possible. Landmarks,
ocean marks keep shifting but keep
coming on. That school of whales
has been here, near here before,
and our insides leap riding
the back of that great water-breaking
shape, carting his own scenery
with him. The sun careens
around the earth at a breath-taking speed
to that old hide.
                    Every dawn is a drama
played by light, surfacing surprise,
streams of color dragged across your eye
balls. That dark island which grew
in you, which you have spewed up to indent
the horizon, now has a golden hummock
to show you that it cares. No,
to show you light is all that matters
after all ("hit it with the baby," and
anyone in the theatre would walk that beam
of spot light to the stage,) and that is what
we search for, after all, not oceans,
islands, not this continual wandering about
backstage, banging our heads on the dressing room door,
but the moment on our inner stage
when we have "hit it with the baby"
          and light blooms.

*Patricia Monaghan*

## THE GREENPEACE SCIENTIST DEBATES THE ESKIMO WHALER

1.
Flutes: whales respond to their sound
with intense pleasure. I have
heard a killer sing across
a huge bay like a choir.
What genius teaches art to
ocean mammals? Our flutes called,
the whales sang back. There's much we
do not know about these songs.
But we know this: it's time
we learned to share the planet.
Whales are living creatures: they're
not metaphors for size and
rareness, they're not dreams of lost
freedom. If, one day, whales are
not to be a memory,
it's up to you. Help us stop
the slaughter. Or can you face
the vast ocean's silences?

2.
Last winter we had no meat
after November except
what we bought with foodstamps. Would
we kill our culture? You say
this year we take no bowhead.
And I say back to you: we
watch the pack ice with slitted
glasses of bone. Our hunters
sing in silence to the whale
the melody of hunger.
I say, we will sing again
this June as whales are struck
and landed. I say we'll raise
the ribs of the greater one
and dance beneath. I tell you,
we will take forty-four whales.
Our culture will not die. We
will not starve: I promise it.

*Geoff Peterson*

## THE RAPTURE

At death of Makin-Meang
the spirit walks north by the shore
and Nakaa the Gate Watcher
tugs on his net.

To the south the Porpoise Caller
enters his hut, his sleep
runs the vast line keening out.
Porpoise enters the dream's blue margin,
the dream gives suck.
*Teirake teirake* he cries.
Crooning we run to meet him when the dream
slams shut.
       Hug my porpoise belly
he pleads hug me to this sound
to feast it fills me.
       And we eat him

See him on the blue wind
pig-eyed and bleeding.
Spear-struck goes the prayer —
of childbirth, false labor, a fall.
Nakaa spreads the rumor at our feet,
Nakaa the sand the net going out,
the coming in is Nakaa.
How well you keep the gate
its water lapping up seems everywhere
says Porpoise.

       Let us make death
a hut for you to go to
in our sleep.
Your walk draws the blue coast
north, blue wind intersecting.
Nakaa the point the cove monger
tempts you with youth.
Nakaa son of a bitch, Nakaa
struts his chant this blue line
desolate in the west.
Here we sing it we call it out
by name, crooning west we come from west
we look to.
       The Porpoise comes

*Will Inman*

## A DOLPHIN WAY
## from "To Change Our Cast of Mind"

1.
in another age   between time of trees
                         and time of high ground
i lived my days in ocean,
my nights in beachcaves or in huts under dunes.
in those days i found kin with dolphins —
they recognize me still, though i have forgot our surf
sisterhood, they ride me to the beach when i'm
drowning.
              water is their free space
but i've forgot how to swim, yet dolphins
go with me to the deepest places
if i will accept their joy all the way down

together we enter the giant clam
together we climb the coils of the conch
their joy defends me from the maws of shellfish
their innocence is no stranger
      to the lava-thrusts of Poseidon's thighs
they brook no sharks
they herd mackerel for my hungry nets
they kiss my feet to fins
they make love with me like underwater meteors
i had forgotten that ocean in me, under, i tell you
these things: if you will come with me
dolphins will comrade you
they've been awaiting us for a long time

they dance all the way, they will teach us
moonleaps and suncoils, they will bring us secrets
buried in us when deserts drove us to ocean
they know us from when we forgot who we were — oh
that surf still rocks in our skulls, now
we are barnacled with dust, but dolphins
hold the sea-strings of our pulses, they
know who we are,
under

hoofs of blue sky dance my eyebones
fins of green ocean drum my ears
all over, i am wounds toward wholeness
out of my ribs a child and a beast and a whale
lick salt at the surfroot of dunes
i weep and wrestle for god's angry rainbows
i force night down my throat till dolphins
tell me i am ready to dive

2.
now that dolphins leap your doubt
distance with fierce currents of joy,
come with me down into the desolate cities of our young,
search out the lost children, bored alike
by starvation and comfort of empty parents

are they less our sisters and brothers than dolphins
oh they too will teach us if we
will help them rediscover what they already
know:
      hunger and boredom have punished them
for what they are not
              they crowd our prisons and our wars
it is in our own ribs they
suffocate harboring desperate escapes and murders
because we will not hear
ourselves
      let alone our young
            have we forgotten
our own cries as we forgot our diving
fins

never forget dolphins, they
will lead us joyous down into our depths
oh steep where trust wakes fresh tides
beating in our ribs.

*Albert Goldbarth*

## DOLPHIN: MONOLOGUE & SONG
## from "Mammalogues"

Once I approached you. What you call
a hand was perforating
water. Then you reached land
and walked. But the hand knew.

*Now I will sing you the dolphin song:*
*The sperm is a fish.*
*The fish is a lung.*

Sometimes, my eyes go opaque
as scale. And then the clarifying rush
in of air shocks, and
quickens. I could envy you this.

*A fish out of water is dead*
*Or is Man. The blood's where it ends.*
*The sea's where it began.*

And I understand it as the link.
The distinction between sea and blood
is a subtle chemistry neither you nor I know
with the finesse of shark.

*The ocean's inside, and heart*
*Moves its tides. Under the moon*
*Men swim into their brides.*

So we're both warm. Sometimes
you give a touch that's warm,
one in a series. I'm
a touch. That could be the division.

*Inside a woman the coming-home calls.*
*The cunt is a gill.*
*The cock hears and swells.*

It's this: I tried it. Once, I tried
a thumb, that theory of opposition.
But then I decided to build my city with
no tool but a spine.

*The ear is a shell.*
*To make love makes oars.*
*Head next to head, the birth-water roars.*

And I live here. We
live here, and signal, and rub
up love, and reason,
in tactility. Look . . .

*Some are born single,*
*Some tied close by skin.*
*But always, in brine, everyone has a twin.*

If the gray of the brain, in its mother blood
could fashion its body as like itself
as possible . . . Look, we
do envy the "wheel." but I'm saying . . .

*He knows you. He knows that you dream*
*Of the splash. You know him by breathing.*
*The lung is a fish.*

You say what could be done
without hands? We say this
is what hand could do
freed from the body.

*Carol Berge*

# GREY, OR TURTLE, SONG

There are just so many ways a sea-turtle can show affection. Or, for
that matter, emotion of any kind. On the assumption that sea-turtles
have or could show, emotions, as we use the term. Thousands of folks
at Marine World every year, more all the time. Admiring the seals as
they balance beach-balls and wave their flippers in what looks like
applause. Considering it a distinct possibility that dolphins can
"speak," or at any rate communicate to humans on their level. A
certain patronizing attitude. A couple I know keeps a sea-turtle (actu-
ally, a turtle from the Amazon River region, so it's a river turtle) in a
tank, in their apartment. It's been there and alive for some fifteen
years now. There's no way to tell what kind of time-measurement
works in the life of a turtle; since some of them live for 500 years, the
idea of time as we see it must be relative. The turtle is made with fins
rather than feet, and navigates the length and breadth of that tank in
about half a minute. Or what must seem like no time at all. The other
night, there was a party at that apartment, and, as usual, the turtle got
a lot of attention, especially from those who'd never seen it, because it
is "unusual-looking," that is, it doesn't much resemble what our
conditioned and ordinary concept of a turtle would lead us to expect: it
has no little feet, pointing inward to leave tracks on tropical sand, no
round shell to paint palm trees &c. on . . . its very expression, if that is
the word, begs for anthropomorphic metaphor. It is at that point that
the question comes to mind, human mind that is: how does this sea-
turtle or river turtle express itself, if indeed it does. It is limited by
more than its environment. First, certainly, there is the ovoid shell,

then the shape of the aquarium, then the physiological construction of the head and facial structure. There was a woman at that party who looked very much like that turtle. She passed close by the tank and the turtle pivoted clumsily on one end of the tank, the left end as we saw it, and seemed to hurry toward the end where she stood, and moved to the top of the water. and veered on its long neck toward that woman. She, passing, stopped, and put out her hand toward the tank — the turtle. The head of the turtle, as it came out of the water, pierced the skin of the water crisply and came toward her in a direct gesture. How could the turtle make itself understood. What does it have available to communicate whatever it is — to that woman? "Woman," we call her, meaning the female of a certain species. Yet her nose is shaped much like a snubby version of the turtle's snout. Neither of them has what the rest of us would call much of a chin. Her neck is long and viable, rising up from her grey, strong gown, her eyes grey like its, and her basic overall coloration a silvery grey, like its. The turtle took her finger in its mouth. Catherine and the turtle stared at each other for that moment. They were in love. As much with the Self as with the Other — as is often the case. The moment passed, as all such moments pass. Some barriers are not meant to be breached, more's the pity. Out of sync, they were, in time — she, after all, is descended from the turtle. Nowhere is it written that love is relative to time. All of the dimensions have been explored except that — and the one across species.

*Judith Moffett*

## BALLADE
## from "Key West"

The reptile brain is cold and small,
No space, no need for judgment there.
Watch. In the deepest Turtle Kraal
A monstrous head pokes up for air,
Lairpet of Grendel's, chased from lair
To scare up dinner. Jaws of dread
Gasp open. Eyes of earthenware
Identify. The loggerhead

Lunges on cue; the guide will trawl
A chunk of rotten lobster where
He'll strike. Abruptly I recall
The moth aflutter on the bare
Floorboards, the little lizard's stare,
Fixed, from the threshold, how it sped
Across the varnish . . . yes. Compare?
Identify? the loggerhead

Who wallows, tries to climb the wall,
Whose ton of crushing-power can tear
A man in chunks and eat him all,
Whose fins thrash up the mal de mer,
Who now, with all that force to spare,
Crushes the bait and sinks like lead.
A blonde child shrieks. These kinds of scare
Identify the loggerhead

And lizard with its charming flare
Round as a flannel tongue and red.
Look long, think well before you dare
Identify the loggerhead.

*Donald Finkel*

## MMMMMM

---

*I am completely vulnerable to him and he pushes and shoves my legs and feet, and quite pathetically tries to satisfy himself. I can feel his mounting frustration.*

Margaret Howe, in *The Mind of the Dolphin* by John Lilly

All night the lady tosses in her sodden sheets
shedding her own salt tears on the briny pillow
all night Peter's tail whap-whaps the water
restless wavelets twitch the flimsy curtain
uneasy shadows flounder on the ceiling
her ankles sting from the nicks of his teeth
but for all her human guile and feminine wit
it's Peter who teaches and Margaret who's taught

playing, he lets his favorite ball
roll back in his mouth, parting his teeth
in a permanent smile, as if to say
*Come I won't hurt you*

*I stand very still, legs slightly apart, and Peter slides his mouth gently over my skin. His mouth opens all the way and he begins up and down my leg. Then the other leg.*

a month of this salty courtship
till one evening, in the second moon
of their togethering, he lets the ball
slip from his mouth entirely
and, rolling on his side
approaches.

MARGARET:  MMMMMM MMAGRIT *Yes! Yes! (clapping) That's*
PETER:     *(softly)   Mxx   xxx*
MARGARET:  *an EM. Let's do it again. Say . . . MMAGRIT*
PETER:     *mxxxxxxxxxx*

*Richard Harteis*

## THE DOLPHINS

Who hasn't
at some point
succumbed.
Their sleek
intelligence,
their wit.
The charm of a boy
on a dolphin.

Since men first tried
the dark oceans,
these silver animals
have burst into blue air
unexpected as friendship.
And lonely sailor boys
might strip to imitate
the sport these brothers took
in each other's shining bodies.

In dark caves
behind the bars
pretty boys
beautiful men
still swim in their
pleasure like dolphins
at death in the seas.

Nothing avails
their animal innocence.
Extinction is
the unnatural act.

The dolphin's song
fades like the ocean
noise trapped
in a conch shell, the last
shy smile of a boy
drowned at sea.

III
Slaughter

*William Stafford*

## A MORNING

From high tide in the night a dead
sea lion explains itself on the wide beach —
folded back arms, drooping petals of feet,
one loud little rifle hole back of the mild
sleeping head. The world tilts back;
the sea returns. When stars pull their wires
tonight those dead eyes will move, and waves
make the deep song. Dunes will come
whispering back. Feathery grass will try
its long dim roots, a new version.

*Alan Britt*

## THE BABY HARP SEAL

When the baby harp seal looks up,
its eyes are indeed two perfectly round, black pools
of oil.
When the baby harp seal looks up
its lovable and mysterious eyes
begin to pierce the usual boredom,
so innocent and so terrible.
When the hunters come,
their boots grind the snow into a pavement
of grief.
The long wooden handle overhead,
the club comes down
then again and again
as it must,
to stop all movement
in the helpless ball of fur.
When the hunters come,
scythes of blood begin to drip
from the sky.
The newsreporter with remote camera unit ascends,
and when the baby harp seal looks up
the souls of thousands of sad people
are suddenly electrocuted, and left crying
privately
in dimly lit living rooms.

*Michael Benedikt*

## OF SEALS AND OUR SMILES

The last time they did any harm to anyone was 1000's of years ago; —
    Therefore we catch them & cut them up into coats,
Their frolicsomeness, too, sliced up by contemptuous human analysis;
    Yes; to the binoculars of the man in the dinghy, as if in a magnifying-
    glass
The seals as they cavort, it seems, tend to read like some pre-
    prepared, allegedly amusing, & gloriously convenient gloss
*On how the weak are only here on this our sad planet to be hurt.*

The last time they did any harm to anyone was 1000's of years ago; —
    therefore we find them in the circus, like particularly hilarious
    characters, forced by us to be terribly funny
On multicolored stands, noses pressed up against old autohorns,
& Falling all over themselves, performing "God Bless America," or (yes)
    "The Internationale"
Half-starved for a half-rotten fish, & the target
Of our ancient disrespect, secret loathing, & still only half-hidden
    contempt
*Since the weak are only here on this our sad planet to be hurt.*

Gaze, gaze again, oh Humans of Goodwill, upon more of what even our
    own dear children typically can see—examine, for example, the sight
    of a seal coming out of its little white hut in the zoo; and then, as it
    raises its remaining nose to sniff the city air
Slipping on a banana-peel; &, oh yes, let's examine some reactions to that
    as the creature falls
*For as long as the weak are only here on this our sad planet to be hurt.*

*Naomi Lazard*

## THE VANISHING MAN

He puts down the book he was reading
about the slaughter of seals for their skins,
the images frozen in his brain
like their blood on the snow. Baby seals
flayed still alive, squirming
with their bodies a little. The flippers
crossed on their breasts, the babies
bleating, the drone of a helicopter just above
for aerial photographs.
                                    He leaves
his hermetically sealed apartment, the furniture,
rows of books, the hi fi, the piano,
dirty dishes, cigarettes. It is a soundless
day lying in light, stone shade, water
far away, no wind. It is a day
like the elevator going up and down.

The book is in his brain, the baby seals
still alive, the seal cows still trying
to suckle the flayed raw bodies. The snow
is terrible with blood. They are all dead
by this time, dying again and again
in his brain, the babies with their flippers
appealing not to be hurt. The hunters
murder again and again in his brain
that is flaming with the small cries
of the babies.
                        The helicopter circles,
the photographer clicks, bent double,
picture after picture. The book
opens and closes. He is the litany
of the helicopter, he is the photographer,
the hunter, the cow seal, the baby seal
with his flippers bent, begging,
over his breast.

The sun rays slash his eyes. "Forgive me,"
he whispers to no one, hurrying away from the book.
"Forgive me," he murmurs and sees quite close
to the ground, one webbed fin thrusting
into the world and the head tilted at an odd angle,
face puckered in wonder. The man confronts
the body without a skin. The animal's nostrils
quiver. "We two are abroad in this pitiless
place, alone. What shall we do?"
"My tall friend," says the animal. "No!"
cries the man. "Follow me," whispers the seal.
"To the red snow?" "Yes."

There is no other life anymore,
only himself in an endless morning,
and the seal. His mouth moves as he glides
past the drugstore, the barbershop, anywhere.
His brain gasps as he sheds the skin of his life
to join the seals. He goes with great strides
northward, past the high tide mark, like a boat.
He's gone. He is going. With his hand clasping
the bay seal's flipper, as long as his brain
lasts, as long as the red stains the snow.

*Marge Piercy*

## ANOTHER COUNTRY

When I visited with the porpoises
I felt awkward, my hairy
angular body sprouting its skinny
grasping limbs like long mistakes.
The child of gravity and want I sank
in the salt wave clattering with gadgets,
appendages. Millennia past
they turned and fled back to the womb.
There they feel no fatigue but slip
through the water caressed and buoyed up.
Never do they sleep but their huge brains
hold life always; turning it like a pebble
under the tongue, and lacking practice, death
comes as an astonishment.

In the wide murmur of the sea they fear
little. Together they ram the shark.
Food swims flashing in schools.
Hunger is only a teasing, endured
no longer than desired. Weather
is superficial decoration; they rise
to salute the thunder, romping their tails.

They ride through pleasure and plenty
secure in a vast courtesy
firm enough to sustain a drowning man.
Nothing is said bluntly.
All conversation is a singing,
all telling alludes to and embodies
minute displacements in epic,
counter-epic, comic opera, or the four hundred
forty-one other genres they recognize
as current. Every exchange comes
as aria, lyric, set piece, recitativo,
and even a cry for help is couched
in a form brief and terse,
strict as haiku.

Greed has no meaning when no one
is hungry. Thus they swim toward
us with broad grins and are slaughtered
by the factory ships
that harvest the tuna like wheat.

*Stephen Dunn*

# HAVING LOST ALL CAPACITY

> *"I am a man and count*
> *nothing human alien to me."*
> — Terence

Today I read how Japanese fishermen
lured thousands of dolphins ashore,
slaughtering them because they eat fish
the fishermen want to catch and sell,
and tomorrow it'll be people once again
mutilating other people, and there'll come a time
when I'll just sit there turning the pages
having lost all capacity for horror
and so much that is human
will be alien to me I'll want to kill
all the killers. I'll walk past my wife
with a kitchen knife and out the door
into streets where others like me
will be slashing at wind and shadows . . .
until the first ripped neck.

I hear everything gets calmer then.
After the first time with a girl I remember
smelling my fingers and then tasting them,
and that's what I hear the first righteous
murder smells and tastes like, only better,
and with the headlines from a week of tabloids
in my mouth I'll know what the end
of the world tastes like, *irresistible,*
and that's all I can think about
here in my room, the sons of bitches,
the bastards!

*Alan Dugan*

## UNTITLED POEM

One used to be able to say
what Seneca said to Nero:
"However many people you kill
you can never kill your successor."
But now the joke may not
be necessarily true: we might
have done it already. So let's
remember what the poet Oppian said:
"The hunting of Dolphins is immoral
and the man who wilfully kills them
will not only not go to the gods
as a welcome sacrifice, or touch
their altars with clean hands, but will
even pollute the people under his own roof."

*Diana Der Hovanessian*

## WHALE

I am trying to say
wait, but the gasp
catches, and is shoved
back. Wait.

The only thing
that separates us
is language. Wait.

In my dream I am caught
in a huge mountain
of blubber.

And cannot escape.
Words stick into
my side like harpoons.

*Norman Rosten*

## BABY WHALE IN CAPTIVITY

I miss the sea most of all.
It took me some weeks
to realize the whitewashed pool
was not my true home:
the water too transparent,
without mystery or danger,
and my mother's shadow
no longer moved about me.
How I missed her hovering
bulk, her weight of
tenderness! I once slept
in peace beneath her fins.

Then somewhere within me
her loss, like a wound,
opened and spread
and pulled me away
in a tide darker than the sea.

*Dorothy Ward*

## WHALE

In the morning
he calls her.
Nuzzles the warmth of the water
    as if her wake,
then listens
to his song
        float to the surface
like a faltering fish.

Sunlight
seasons the tank with spring.
He dives deep —
        skimming the glass,
                smooth
as her belly
and thickens to the thought.

Searching her heat,
he circles to press the pane,
    then circles
        to press
            the pane —
snatching swells
    to tighten each loop.
Straining to seed.

He burns,
searing the salt water
with his spray.
He nestles the wall,
    raw for her.
And his stain
    echoes through the pool
like a cry.

*Robert Gibb*

## THE FLENSERS

Torn out of the sea
Like an arm
From a bloodied socket,
Grist and ball-joint,
The whale collapses —

Its great bulk slumped
Upon the slippery yard
To wait for defacement
Beyond the awful
Abbreviation of the flukes,
The tangled, ripped tongue.

The slim and elegant V
Of the genital slit waits
Waist-high and vulnerable
As though even sodomy
Might spark something
Like love from the grim
Unwavering motions
Of the flensers.

Anonymous men,
Faces like fingernails
And alike as ants.
From the distance
They look like skaters
With their long, hockey-
Stick shaped knives,
Chasing a clot of a puck,
Stripping, peeling,
Coring the whale down
To the shy, feminine bones.

They follow a routine
Ritual of thought,
Automatic as tying shoes.
Each act a simple step
In an intricate order,
Unvaried as a recipe.

They repeat it endlessly,
The series down to nothing.
*Pièce de resistance:*
Pungent, perfect,
Gleamingly dead.

*Margo Stever*

## ASCENSION

> *It takes seven strong men*
> *to drag the six-foot heart*
> *of a blue whale*
> *across the deck of a whaling ship.*
> — Faith McNulty

Beads of sweat well up on the sea-
stained faces of the seven men
who bear the still warm heart
of the blue whale to the boiling vats.
The men are deliverers; they tug,
rip, tear the heart
across the deck of the seething pots.
But their hands stick to surfaces
like fly paper, and recoil,
the red matter teething into fingers
as if leaching out the blood.
Ventricles, gaping mouths,
stand ajar; red smoke rises
in the darkening mist.
Sea wind raps against crevices,
something trying to get back in,
tapping out an aberrant beat,
an unknown code, and something whines,
long and low, a sea moan.
To lift a six-foot heart
requires a crane, and as the last
inch of the once raised organ
recedes into the stewing vats,
dismembered parts of the heart
ascend and billow over the deck.
Seven men inhale the scalding vision,
their own hearts slackening with each breath.

*Raymond Henri*

## THE WHALE
## *from "The Reincarnations"*

Before disaster went down to every sea
I was content to let impoverished
Japanese villagers taste occasional
triumph over one of us.
That could help keep alive
seven villages, bearing off
flensed sections of a beached carcass,
using everything we had to give
for food, shelter, boats,
implements and warmth —
wasting nothing.

I even could excuse New Englanders,
desperate for salvation,
who read their bibles
by my dying light
and, later, those who sought baleen
to rein in their women's
excess blubber.

But when oared boats gave way
to factory ships; hand-thrown harpoons
to instrument-guided explosives —
when winged searchers
could sight me from above
and listening gear could sound
me in my depths,
I knew that I was doomed.

I prayed for change.

*Michael Gregory*

## HUEVOS MEXICANOS

The full moon gapes onto the beach at Nexpa
as shadows of men with machetes and children
with empty baskets pass under the palms to where
the last great sea turtles lay eggs the rich
and ignorant will eat tomorrow in Acapulco.

*Jan Goodloe*

## SEA TURTLES

On the summer beaches of Trinidad
and Tobago, Tortuguero and the Florida
Keys, sea turtles do this dance.
The male waits in the shallows
to mate: hooks thumb claws over the female's
carapace, onto the soft flesh between
neck and shoulder. The female alone lumbers
ashore; cupped flippers scoop out sand.
She vents a clutch of parchment eggs into
the hollow, covers it with delicate
motions. Her flippers track
a halfmoon path back to the sea.

Hatchlings erupt at dusk or in
the dark. Their wriggling loosens sand
from the roof of the nest. Bottom hatchlings
trample the fallen sand, the level rises.
They ascend and scuttle on rubbery legs
toward water. Hawkbills, loggerheads,
flatbacks, leatheries, greens and ridleys.
Poachers and predators lurk behind dunes
or wait in slender green seagrass. Eggs,
meat, oil, and shell tempt the omnivorous.
A hundred million years of history tumble
into water heavy and silverwhite as mercury.

*Edmund Pennant*

## DRY TORTUGAS

A middle-aged turtle allowed himself
to sink whenever the boat
eased toward him. Why do men
whisper behind weapons?
Five times he disappeared
at the right moment; but then
they scooped up the entire sea
under him, and clubbed him
with sunbeams on the undershell
among ropes and nets.

The subsequent history of this case
is conventional, ending in
a commutation of sentence for
the hunters, because the face
of the turtle being comic-saturnine,
it is easier to see die, than, say,
the face of the man facing
the firing squad, poise and puzzlement
or terror in the doomed visage
setting a snelled hook in the mind
that must make ready, aim and fire.
Or worse, the face in the black bag.

A sea turtle, dead, needs
a ghost sea to haunt us in;
but even the seas are menaced
by indifference, whether they rise
or fall to actual moons
or imagined light contrived by men.

*Donald Kummings*

## NEW PROVIDENCE ISLAND, BAHAMAS

Pallid, bloated as a fish, the day swells with heat.
Beneath a lard-white sun
the guide enters a whitewashed building,
strays along walls.
We bend above a concrete tank of brooding water.
I peer down at sea turtles, filmy green,
adrift in a squat sea.
Excrement bobs in the tank like kelp.
In a dark nook at the rear of the market
two men play a game with plum seed dice,
while one man, in back of a snailtrack of dirt, leans on a broom.
Nearby, the guide extends a blue, enamel basin,
chipped, heavy with its pale strips of sweet, wet meat.
But I see and have seen simply two enormous turtles.
A restaurant has ordered them,
two which awhile ago were wrestled from the tank,
hurled out into the stark, dusty universe of this floor,
now in immense exhaustion,
heaving, stifling, drowning in air:
dark, salt-caked eyes, profoundly old, straining like the sea,
jaws, horny and toothless, giving off gasp and suck,
faded yellow bony shells upturned
and, where spiked, blackened by a fist of flies,
leathery limbs extending in a desperate, slow shiver.

The hands of an overhead fan revolve like a clock.
Weak, I lean toward light and shadow
struggling at the door.

Now an iodine sun,
dark blood clabbered on the gills of fish-colored sky.
I lurch in a crowd.
The tourists are taking pictures of passion fruit,
In my ear, far off, I hear the rush and hum of fluids,
the pulse of currents.
I feel, far in, a deep sea floor upon which something is asway.
Its form (delicate as the roar of a seashell)
dilates like a membranous sac, pitches,
tosses on a fibrous stalk,
labors in distended blackness.

Something would come forth, would make a gesture strange
and green as motions of a seaweed hand.
Something human would emerge from original silence
and speak with the clarity of water,
would grope toward birth,
would, into stark, bright air, astonished, rise.
The wharf is slippery with the eyes of bonefish.

*Duane Locke*

## SEA TURTLE

Near St. Augustine there is a shore of rocks,
limestone and coral.
An emerald, silver-wrinkled water flows over
orange-red, sea urchin sand.
                              The last time
I visited these rocks,
                              a dead sea turtle
was floating. On his neck a deep gash as if cut by
a motorboat.
              The sand I held in my hand wilted
as if it were a leaf,
                              and turned into the brown shape
of an aborted, almost born star.

## SEA TURTLE

Before me is a sea turtle
  bleached shell
  adult green turtle
The poacher's prints washed by the sea
  turtle on her back
  shell cut away
  while the animal breathes
  knife blade
  She cannot roll over
  Dawn at her tail
  Vultures
  circle     swoop down
  that's that

Turtle meat: $25
Turtle eggs: 4¢

  Horseflies across the corpse

"If the turtle meat can be sold
outside the country, prices
are multiplied"

  Water at high tide
  pulls the shell home
  where we got our start

  Sweet sea     bone-sipper
  marrow-mother

  a turtle floats back
  inside you
  enters your salt veins

rhythm of water rhythm of land

  heartbeat

Rugged wanderer who shall have us
again and again    have us    have us

*IV*
*Elegy*

*Stanley Kunitz*

## THE WELLFLEET WHALE

1.
You have your language too,
   an eerie medley of clicks
      and hoots and trills,
location-notes and love calls,
   whistles and grunts. Occasionally,
      it's like furniture being smashed,
or the creaking of a mossy door,
   sounds that all melt into a liquid
      song with endless variations,
as if to compensate
   for the vast loneliness of the sea.
      Sometimes a disembodied voice
breaks in, as if from distant reefs,
   and it's as much as one can bear
      to listen to its long mournful cry,
a sorrow without name, both more
   and less than human. It drags
      across the ear like a record
running down.


2.
No wind. No waves. No clouds.
   Only the whisper of the tide,
      as it withdrew, stroking the shore,
a lazy drift of gulls overhead,
   and tiny points of light
      bubbling in the channel.
It was the tag-end of summer.
   From the harbor's mouth
      you coasted into sight,
flashing news of your advent,
   the crescent of your dorsal fin
      clipping the diamonded surface.
We cheered at the sign of your greatness
   when the black barrel of your head
      erupted, ramming the water,
and you flowered for us
   in the jet of your spouting. .

3.
All afternoon you swam
    tirelessly round the bay,
        with such an easy motion,
the slightest downbeat of your tail,
    an almost imperceptible
        undulation of your flippers,
you seemed like something poured,
    not driven; you seemed
        to marry grace with power.
And when you bounded into air,
    slapping your flukes,
        we thrilled to look upon
pure energy incarnate
    as nobility of form.
        You seemed to ask of us
not sympathy, or love,
    or understanding,
        but awe and wonder.

That night we watched you
    swimming in the moon.
        Your back was molten silver.
We guessed your silent passage
    by the phosphorescence in your wake.
        At dawn we found you stranded on the rocks.

4.

There came a boy and a man
  and yet other men running, and two
    schoolgirls in yellow halters
and a housewife bedecked
  with curlers, and whole families in beach
    buggies with assorted yelping dogs.
The tide was almost out.
  We could walk around you,
    as you heaved deeper into the shoal,
crushed by your own weight,
  collapsing into yourself,
    your flippers and your flukes
quivering, your blowhole
  spasmodically bubbling, roaring.
    In the pit of your gaping mouth
you bared your fringework of baleen,
  a thicket of horned bristles.
    When the Curator of Mammals
arrived from Boston
  to take samples of your blood
    you were already oozing from below.
Somebody had carved his initials
  in your flank. Hunters of souvenirs
    had peeled off strips of your skin,
a membrane thin as paper.
  You were blistered and cracked by the sun.
    The gulls had been pecking at you.
The sound you made was a hoarse and fitful bleating.

What drew us to the magnet of your dying?
  You made a bond between us,
    the keepers of the nightfall watch,
who gathered in a ring around you,
  boozing in the bonfire light.
    Toward dawn we shared with you
your hour of desolation,
  the huge lingering passion
    of your unearthly outcry,
as you swung your blind head
  toward us and laboriously opened
    a bloodshot, glistening eye,
in which we swam with terror and recognition.

5.
Voyager, chief of the pelagic world,
   you brought with you the myth
      of another country, dimly remembered,
where flying reptiles
   lumbered over the steaming marshes
      and trumpeting thunder lizards
wallowed in the reeds.
   While empires rose and fell on land,
      your nation breasted the open main,
rocked in the consoling rhythm
   of the tides. Which ancestor first plunged
      head-down through zones of colored twilight
to scour the bottom of the dark?
   You ranged the North Atlantic track
      from Port-of-Spain to Baffin Bay,
edging between the ice-floes
   through the fat of summer,
      lob-tailing, breaching, sounding,
grazing in the pastures of the sea
   on krill-rich orange plankton
      crackling with life.
You prowled down the continental shelf,
   guided by the sun and stars
      and the taste of alluvial silt
on your way southward
   to the warm lagoons,
      the tropic of desire,
where the lovers lie belly to belly
   in the rub and nuzzle of their sporting;
      and you turned, like a god in exile,
out of your wide primeval element,
   delivered to the mercy of time.
      Master of the whale-roads,
let the white wings of the gulls
   spread out their cover.
      You have become like us,
disgraced and mortal.

*Ellen Bryant Voigt*

## SUICIDES

Ink blot, sperm on a slide, a squirm
of minnows from the helicopter's
view, the whales have beached.
All day the volunteers have poked
and prodded, but they will not
turn back. Behind them their salty
element foams and rushes: how often
they sounded the dark layers,
past the lacy skeletons of coral,
the squid preparing his black cloak
for a getaway — the ease of gliding,
motion in the midst of motion,
through water! the pull of water
as they stored breath and dove again
and again, looking for bottom, down
to where fish blossom among the sponges
and fossils, where the plants are meat-
eating and sexual, where the ocean
opens to cold drafts that clamp
an iron vise against the skull.

Graceful in water, they labor now
toward palmetto and tufted
hillocks, the hot sun bleaching
and drying out. Their fins dig into
something solid, the broad flukes
spade, then anchor in the sand.

## AÚN (XXIV)

La Ballenera de Quintay, vacía
con sus bodegas, sus escombros muertos,
la sangre aún sobre las rocas, los
huesos de los monárquicos cetáceos,
hierro roído, viento y mar, el graznido
del albatros que espera.

Se fueron las ballenas: a otro mar?
Huyeron de la costa encarnizada?
O sumergidas en la suave lodo
de la profundidad piden castigo
para los oceánicos chilenos?

Y nadie defendió a las gigantescas!

Hoy, en el mes de Julio
resbalo aún en el aceite helado
se me van los zapatos hacia el Polo
como si las presencias invisibles
me empujaran al mar,
y una meloncolia grave como el invierno
va llevando mis pies
por la deshabitada Ballenera.

*Pablo Neruda*

## AUN (XXIV)

The whaling grounds of Quintay, empty
with its caverns, the debris of the dead,
blood still up on the rocks, the
bones of the undersea monarchs,
rusted iron, wind and sea, the scream
of the albatross waiting.

The whales have gone: to another sea?
Did they flee from this coast of carnage?
Or lying submerged in the soft bottom sands
do they from the depths ask retribution
for all Chilean sea creatures?

And nobody defended the leviathans!

Today, in the month of July,
I still slip around in frozen oil.
My shoes float away from me toward the South Pole
as if the ghosts of the whales
draw me toward the sea
and a grave melancholy sets in like winter
directing my steps
along the deserted whaling grounds.

*translated by Carlos Reyes*

*Adrienne Wolfert*

## THE SUICIDES

Red is the sea, the red sea flecked with white
and bobbing here and there, the fish, like buoys,
whip their bellies on the jagged rock
until they bleed the blood salt ocean blood,
driven by unsubtle self-destruction
to the irresistible.

King of the sea, the whale, who worsted
man his fiercest enemy, air-breathing
fountain, the Great Fish
swallower of Jonah, lamp to dark ages,
food and furrier to emperors, symbolic
challenger of bitter seamen, who tipped
vessels with a dive, gigantic
dolphin, why fling
your sleek well-fatted body
on this cross?

Mammal, then,
kin to Man who slays
his generations in a suicide
and worships One who by his own will
died,
bearing in your belly,
life,
you think you own it.

*Peter Meinke*

## THE DEATH OF THE PILOT WHALES

Every few years down at the Florida keys,
where bones chew the water like mad dogs
and spit it bubbling out on yellow sand,
the sea darkens, and we crane toward the skies,
toward the airplanes casting their shadows,
but there are no planes and those dark shadows
are not shadows, but mark the silent forms
of pilot whales charging the shore like wild
buffalo charging a train, driving toward
reef and sand till the foam sprays red
below the rainbow stretching from sea to land.

The fierceness of it all, unstoppable,
those broad flukes churning the water, that buried
brain and heart set inflexibly on their last
pulsing, the energy and beauty of all that
flesh turning away from its cold fathomless
world, like the negative of some huge
lemming following God knows whose orders
in a last ordered chaos of frantic obedience
stronger than love. With what joy and
trembling they hunch up the beach,
shred themselves on shoals, what sexual
shudders convulse them at that sweet moment
when they reach — at last! — what
they have burned to meet.

And we, who may be reminded of thoughts
we wish not to think, we tow them back to sea,
cut them open, and they sink.

*Linda Bierds*

## ELEGY FOR 41 WHALES
## BEACHED IN FLORENCE, OREGON, JUNE 1979

> *There was speculation that a parasite in the whales' ears may have*
> *upset their equilibrium and caused them to become disoriented*
>
> *—UPI*

In the warm rods of your ears
forty-one parasites hummed
and you came rolling in
like tarred pilings after a hurricane.
What songs were they piping for you?
What promises did you follow, past the coral
and mussels, and out from the frothy hem
of your world?

These are people.
They dance around you now like hooked marlin.
Some are weeping. Some are trying to pull you back.
Some crouch above your blowholes
and drill their cigarettes into your skin.

All night your teeth are clicking.
All along the beach you are clicking like wind-chimes.
Is the song still piping for you?

This is sand. You cannot swim through it.
These are trees. Those houses on the cliff
are also trees. And the light that blinks
from them now is made from water.
We have a way of reworking the vital:

This is a pit. That was quicklime.
And here is fire.

Margaret Weaver

## STRANDED WHALES

Aground in shallows here, the dark whales lie
Beyond their limits, monstrous and serene.
Beneath the breezes and the sunny sky,
They face high silent dunes and land unseen,
Almost unmoving now. Their skin fades grey
As tide falls and wind dries flesh and sand.
Their wave-borne grace diminishes to sway
Of fins and flukes. They're alien to the end.

Although their eyes reflect us as they die,
We cannot understand what makes them dare.
Refusing the tide's pull, they seem to try
To change the natural laws of blood and air.
Still, in our common pulse, we feel the curl,
The sigh, of waves, and recognize our single world.

*Virginia Linton*

## DIFFERING VIEWS OF A DEAD WHALE

Looming monstrous,
he shone a hide weathered
like an old, rubber boot
in the wrack of the last spring-tide,
his collapsed blowhole puckered, crater-dry,
into a silence beyond size. And some
of the children, who had run shouting
toward sky, around the South Point
to look at him, trampolined in sneakers
off and on the high side of his flank.

Sand profaned
his open jaw, tooth-deep;
and the exposed eye (so seeming small
a light for such a mountain)
lay closed above the sludge of blood
and juices oozing under his head,
staining the deeper sand to rust;
and hissing like a full kettle
shoved back on the stove
with the burner at *low low*.

On this quarter
the children kept their distance
and stared at their own feet.
And even the voracious,
golden-eyed flies buzzed clear
to drone a circular monotone around
the vortex where the great hulk
simmered down to marry with
the age-bound mud.

A variation of gulls hovered: canted
and swung closer, on an indifferent air,
mewling together their feather-light blanket —
deceiving soft as grey cloud-cover —

Calling in,
up the long sea-wind, a congregation of celebrants.

## MAMMALS

Whales are mourning:
warm-blooded brothers
grown vast and graceful
in the sea,

we have heard their voices
as if at night
we woke to a cry from another room:
grief, moving against the wall
and through it,
entering sleep as deep
and whole as ocean
that parts against the blue skin
and fluked tail, then closes.

We have heard their voices;
they course among us
and know our lives
as other rooms, as continents,
upheavals of the ocean floor.

The whales are lamenting,
long calls that billow out
and run toward land,
accreting there like sediment
for man — great-hearted
in his pen of air — from whom
the wind whips such noises.

*Jeanne Voege*

## THE MOURNING
*Westhampton Beach, April 22, 1979*

In cold morning wind we stand on shore
chilled by the sight before us.
Even the sea, swirling red
around the mammoth womb
is hushed.

Wetsuits gleaming black as the whale they flense,
men fight to save the baby.
Deep flesh unfolds . . . thirty tons of it,
chunks like latex pillows
floating the surf
milk white.

Seventeen months, navigating infinite seas;
around explosives; maneuvering
past the long shadows,
this sperm whale carried her last calf
safely . . . until something snagged a tooth.
Wild thrashing, rolls, dives only tightened
the thing — imprisoning, slashing her jaw.
A great dive snapped the rope, but the tangle
remained. Hunger. Gangrene.
And the birthing only one month away!

Here on the sand, the fetus emerges —
thirteen feet long and perfectly formed.
Her skin, black silk gleaming.
Primal memory dark on every face, we huddle,
a small silent crowd.
The still bodies, our kin.

*W. D. Ehrhart*

## THE DEATH OF KINGS

> " . . . *tell sad stories of the death of kings.*"
> — Shakespeare

Giant;
sleek master of the oceans;
you alone command
the land beyond the land.
What else could Jonah have feared
more than the will of God?
Who else could have broken iron Ahab?
Even irreverent Hobbes
paid you the highest respect.

Light gets lost
trying to find you, beating
ever more faintly on your black door,
the black wall of your kingdom.

But the harpooners wait on the surface,
patient as lean cats:
they dare not seek you in your own world,
but they know they do not have to.
In the end they will win,
and we shall have one more kingdom
empty of kings.

*Atanas Slavov*

## GOLIATH

1.
People knew for quite some time
— that is what the experts said —
that whales from the family
of blue whales
had died out because Earth
had passed to a higher geological era
and that particular kind of whale
flourished no more
But it happened that some time ago
Norwegian whalers with bombs and harpoons
undermined a whale like that
and . . .

It became quiet
a 40-ton heart
hidden at the bottom of the ocean millennia ago
stopped
a 22-yard eye
glazed
in front of the TV cameras

Trumpets and drums boomed
Like a carnival procession
from Western through Eastern Europe into Asia
passed the stinking corpse of Goliath
borne upon one hundred squeaking carts with heavy
crooked wheels
pulled by
400 thousand and ten water buffalo

2.
Goliathophiles do not despair
goliathophobes do not rejoice
only know that when they hit Goliath
his mate dove into the ocean depths
carrying within her the fresh semen
of the whale

Let the ocean boil with whaling ships
circus clowns and harpoonists and whalers
the top project of nature is hiding
in the womb down in the water's womb
When the hurricane passes by sail
softly over the waters of the ocean
You will see bubbles of air melting
white and light and transparent as foam
Goliath's mate is breathing down there
while the timid mammals grow in silence
in the womb of their snoozing mother

And the time will come
and then the steady
sound of their hearts is going to break the
silence of the deaf ears of the planet

3.
Never will the planet boom again
alas
I did see Goliath come
he was made of plywood and was small
and he smelled of spoiled linseed oil
and his eyes were cold fried eggs
sunny side up
and he was not a blue whale at all
for blue whales do not thrive any more
and the announcer said over the loudspeaker
that the Japs had killed Goliath's mate

He will drive off stretched on his Renault
and the Goliathomaniacs
of the planet for a quarter only
are going to learn once and for all
that the world will never again boom
in the rhythm
of beastly calm

*Morton Marcus*

## THERE ARE DAYS NOW

There are days now
when I can see the souls of elephants
being towed to heaven.
Soon the trees
will be loosed from their moorings
and sail off like a chorus of Greek women
rigid with grief.
And the whales — soon the whales
will be hulks full of sand.

I am resigned to this,
but with each of these premonitions
there is a crumbling
along the banks of my blood stream.
So if I touch you now,
my friend,
how can it be with my whole hand,
the fat resting firm beneath the palm,
and not with clutching fingers,
as though I had grabbed you in passing
and were holding on?

*May Sarton*

# WHO KNOWS WHERE THE JOY GOES

Who knows where the joy goes
Knows we're killing the dolphins
Somewhere far out to sea.

Caught in the tuna nets
The gentle dolphins drown,
They, no man's enemy.
(Go down grace, go down
Freedom.)

Who wakes from a nightmare
Hearing a faint scream
Knows terror at work
Somewhere far away.
(Go down grace, go down
Gentleness.)

Who weeps without reason
In a sudden seizure
Hears a terrible silence
Half the world away.

Is the last dolphin dying?
Is there no friend left?
Are we here alone?

*Stuart Dybek*

## INSIDE THE TURTLE

My heart once promised
to continue without me,
but my enemies learned patience,
and those who swore they'd rescue me
all died young.

*Simon Perchik*

\*

The turtle once twins, the sea
one wave among many, both kids
to a turtle. For sea. For shore.

It bumped, giggled
inside the shark, taught
fish to laugh: lights
always facing shore.

*Why is my child crying?*

From this sewer
again our street
with undersea tales.

*Land is kinder than the sea,*
answers the driver.

The truck finished them off
but the sea
still meets here
takes from our street
their bones, their odyssey.

*Edward P. Willey*

## SEA TURTLES

Centuries
packed into something indifferent
to everything except its own direction.
A prehistoric lump sculling
sun-streaked salty seas,
created in an age when
all it had to do to justify itself
was grow too large to die.
And now
there isn't time to learn to sing,
to attack when cornered,
or die commercially enough
to sell "T" shirts.
No emergency,
who will even know the difference
afterwards?

*Jack Hand*

## TORTOISE SHELL

There is little to ponder here but absence,
That bright eye smashed,
Which lent a wisdom to his steady sway.
The tortoise has left his shell.
Shall we ask of this empty house
A knowledge of his world,
Where the tight press of flesh closed each corner,
And answered every call of fear —
Except that last —
When a booted foot stopped the clawing forelimbs
And the searching beak found only air,
When his mind, too dull to know itself,
Turned in to greet its death,
That death of which we'd ask
If from his darkness, future knowledge came?

*Aelbert C. Aehegma*

## ANCIENT TURTLE DANCE

E honu, e honu, e pūhā
Turtle, turtle, come up to breathe

For weeks you have not been seen,
for years. Rise out of deep sea
that we may remember your dance
telling of how our land rose
from ocean depths, cracking
into plates as it swelled.
Let brine, let spray break for us
at your shore once more, Grand Old One,
or surely, your dance will be forgotten.

Honu-pe'ekue
          Thick-shelled Turtle
Honu-kahiki
          Foreign Tortoise
Honu-po'o-kea
          White-headed Turtle
Honu-'ea
          Hawksbill Turtle

Especially, you our last, from whose crushed
shells comes our medicine; no more; no
more delight in your dark and your light
amber shell combs for beauty, fans for
leisure; no more dark green meat for luau feast;
no more, for fisher and hunter of today lay waste.
Knowledge, forgotten, missing with their thrust,
knowing not how to fill their mouths. No more

Turtle, turtle, come up to breathe
that we may see your dance, once more.
Last Hawksbill we saw carried a spear in its throat,
its body limp, its head a dirge of flies, alone upon
a black lava coast: its burial pyre, beyond
both of its homes, sacred land, sacred water.

Turtle, turtle, come up to breathe.
We now need to see your red-brown shell.
We need to be reminded of that pattern
upon your back, for new mats need weaving.
We need to prophesy by your heated scales
for our land begins to move again, like you.
We need to smell those distant swells
which carry those mysteries that only sea-life
riding upon your great back usually share.
For great quakes shake, cruel waves breaking,
and our shores sink then rise; volcanoes
steam, throw up curtains of fire, boil on
in an overflow to the breakers. Town and People
all the while spoil land and sea with their greed.

Honu-'ea, Honu-'ea
Honu ne'e pūka āina
       Hawksbill Turtle, Hawksbill Turtle!
       The land moves like a turtle
Holu Honu, Turtle Hula, is it forgotten
E honu, e honu, e pūhā
Turtle, turtle, come up to breathe

*Mariah Burton Nelson*

## THAT SIMPLE, THAT SOPHISTICATED

Sunbathing
flat-naked on an empty beach
I lift my head suddenly to see
a large body floundering in shallow waters.
I leap up, run to the
shark
no — dolphin
and wade out to the slippery mass of blue-gray skin
striped with random lines of deep red
and shallow red
wounds
must sting in ocean salt.

I lay my hands on her bleeding flesh and
— push —
    she wants to beach herself
    is ready to die
    who am I to send her back out to sea
    where hungry fish will eat her alive
but I
— push —

Our two naked bodies struggle
waves lapping the floppy mammal against me
knocking me backwards
bloodying my thighs.
She is big
her tail stronger than any good intent
and the water is on her side.

I talk to this wounded animal
*You'll be O.K.*, I tell her
I try to touch her with my eyes,
*I see your pain*
but love is not enough
to preserve life.

I move away and watch
the force of her dying oblivious
to my futile resistance,
my letting go.

When the ocean lays her battered daughter gently
on the soft sand and recedes

I am still standing knee deep
staring.
The waves slowly slip away
a mother tiptoeing silently
not risking looking back, one more glimpse.

I go to the dolphin
sit cross-legged, stroking her head.
Who should have to die alone?
She ignores me.
I stretch my body next to hers
her length longer than any lover.
I sit up, touch her fin,
pull my hand back.
She lies still
heavy and still as a sleeping sunbather
while I twitch and shift and scuttle around her
the nervous dance of a species distinguished by
written language and
fear of death.

I open my mouth to speak but there is nothing in there.
There is nothing I can do but lie down by her side again,
watching her
pretending she cares.

Already she is changing form.
Her skin begins to dry in the late afternoon
sun, the red slashes widening into
sticky lipstick smiles.

I must remember to breathe
even after she stops.

Just before dawn, when the tide rises
like a deep breath,
dark green waters will cradle
the carcass of this mammal
suck it back out into the fluid vastness
where the dolphin was born.

Now, her dying finished
she will feed the living.
Nature is that simple, that sophisticated.

*Penny Harter*

## WHALE SONG
### Eskimo Cemetery, Alaska

Whalebones arc among white stones.
Bleached old guardians, the great ribs close
like igloos on each grave.

Driven into dirt the bones are still.
One thinks of Jonah and the bellied black,
the hard enfolding.

Sun bounces round the ribs that rim the whole —
They move! They move again, a single ripple,
lean as a xylophone.

The souls of these whales were long ago returned
to the cold seas, the grey sky —
and now this rhythm,
this dance in a white space?

*Robert Bly*

# THE DEAD SEAL NEAR McCLURE'S BEACH

1.

Walking north toward the point, I come on a dead seal. From a few feet away, he looks like a brown log. The body is on its back, dead only a few hours. I stand and look at him. There's a quiver in the dead flesh. My God he is still alive. A shock goes through me, as if a wall of my room had fallen away.

His head is arched back, the small eyes closed, the whiskers sometimes rise and fall. He is dying. This is the oil. Here on its back is the oil that heats our houses so efficiently. Wind blows fine sand back toward the ocean. The flipper near me lies folded over the stomach, looking like an unfinished arm, lightly glazed with sand at the edges. The other flipper lies half underneath. The seal's skin looks like an old overcoat, scratched here and there, by sharp mussel-shells maybe. . .

I reach out and touch him. Suddenly he rears up, turns over. He gives three cries, like those from Christmas toys. He lunges toward me. I am terrified and leap back, although I know there can be no teeth in that jaw. He starts flopping toward the sea. But he falls over, on his face. He does not want to go back to the sea. He looks up at the sky, and he looks like an old lady who has lost her hair.

He puts his chin back on the sand, rearranges his flippers, and waits for me to go. I go.

2.

Today I go back to say goodbye; he's dead now. But he's not — he's a quarter mile farther up the shore. Today he is thinner, squatting on his stomach, head out. The ribs show more — each vertebra on the back under the coat now visible, shiny. He breathes in and out.

He raises himself up, and tucks his flippers under, as if to keep them warm. A wave comes in, touches his nose. He turns and looks at me — the eyes slanted, the crown of his head is like a black leather jacket. He is taking a long time to die. The whiskers white as porcupine quills, the forehead slopes . . . goodbye brother, die in the sound of waves, forgive us if we have killed you, long live your race, your innertube race, so uncomfortable on land, so comfortable in the ocean. Be comfortable in death then, where the sand will be out of your nostrils, and you can swim in long loops through the pure death, ducking under as assassinations break above you. You don't want to be touched by me. I climb the cliff and go home the other way.

# V
# *Reincarnation*

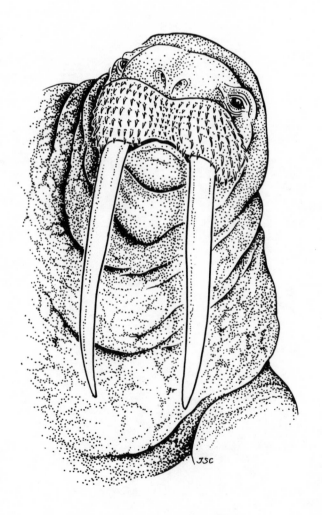

*Kay Boyle*

# REINCARNATION

*From a poem to Samuel Beckett*

There is death in the house.
The spider trapped in the bathtub (slick as a glacier
Its polished heights) is traveler without rope, no thread
                              to unwind, alone
At the end in the slipping and sliding back
Into despair. At the closed pane, the fly curses aloud.
The furtive mouse, steel necklace of trap at its throat,
Is lonelier, greyer, quieter than stone.

May not the process of return to life be so
Reversed that mouse, spider, fly, and even man,
Not having heeded the trilogy of great demands,
Be granted ever higher form until response to what is asked
Is acted out? ("Oh, Jonah he lived in a whale. He made his abode in
That fish's abdomen. Yes, Jonah he lived in a whale.")
And might not fly and spider, mouse and man
Return with the eye of the Blue Whale to offer sight
For the lone search for others of their kind; voyage
Through brine as does the Grey Whale, following seamarks set
Like milestones in the current, gauging the distance to mating
By the stars; return as Bowhead Whale, shifting ice-floes
As easily as scenery in the wings to make a corridor for those
                              who come,
Frolicking, within his spangled wake?

So might transfigured mouse and spider, fly and man
Hear at long last the singing of the Humpback Whale, the arias
Of migration humming and warbling within the ancient flood,
And, hearing, lift on their shoulders a harpooned brother from
                              the tide of blood.

*Nancy Roxbury Knutson*

## SCRIMSHAW

There's something wrong —
the way this whale
this killer
is about to slap
its tail
and upend the boat
spilling the men
into the pointed waves
engraved
on a bone
that very well may be
its own

*Ann Stanford*

## "STOVE BOAT"

The whale has caught this boat
within his jaw and is crushing it.
Six men have fallen into the sea

or struggle away from the teeth
set like anchors in the bony jaw.
Hats, ropes, arms and legs float on the surface.

Oars, snapped in mid-shaft
leap into air or water.
The boat turns sideways

but the rope for the harpoon
still lies coiled in its place
and a sailor clings to the heaving craft.

Two whaleboats move toward the broken center —
their rhythm steady, harpooners wait in the bows —
from the ships that pause at ease in the background

and all is calm round about,
the sea smooth, dented with sun,
the sky clearing over the water.

*Howard Nelson*

## WHALING

The sailors in their berths half-woke
from their creaking sleep
and heard unbelievable music
floating through the ship —
a trumpet falling into the abyss,
long, ecstatic groans, huge ghosts
making love underwater,
the ocean mooing back at the moon.
They thought it was spirits,
but it was more than that —
it was the whales,
sailing through the endless black
water on wide wings,
their mouths hung with dark curtains,
smiling, singing,
through the wood of the hull.
They almost said:
"We forgive everything . . . we are your cousins
who went another way . . . we forgive everything . . . "

*Clarinda Harriss Lott*

## SEA STORY

I find it hard
to explain just why
it moved me so, this summer's
story of a baby white whale
orphaned off the northern coast,
who capsized
white boat after
fat white boat
nuzzling for nipples,

and who, given up
for starved to death,
played for hours
in the surf with
two Nantucket lifeguards
and their thick white towels
(Imagine playing with
a fifteen foot two thousand pound
white dog, they said
of their experience)

yet who among us
has not dived,
starving,
for something to suck —
whose mouth tensed round
for fat white milk
has not lipped
bilge, or brine,
or bled on barnacles,

and lived —
such sour living juice
sustaining us —
to rise
and rise again,
to nip at the flicker
of anything white
on the wine-dark,
womb-dark,
wound-dark sea?

William Doreski

# WHALE-WATCH OFF PORTSMOUTH

The whales burst the chop like roots
worked through topsoil, slick lampblack
harsh in a lawn-green, flustered sea.
Leaning over the rail I stroke
a fin, quick as a first dry kiss,
thick as an old-fashioned slicker.

Cruising off Portsmouth in the fog,
we hardly expected to spot
a seabird, let alone blunder
into the very school of whales
we'd each paid ten dollars to glimpse.

Hardly the behemoths of *Moby Dick*,
still these loutish, gossiping creatures
exude a distinctly mammalian
charm — greater, perhaps, for lack
of menace. Even tongue-in-cheek
Melville must have strained to name "fish"
something he felt such kinship with.

Whale-spotting for fun and profit,
the cruise ship hammers the whitecaps
to raves of meat, while mobbing the deck
we stare transfixed as mannequins,
the loudspeaker's babble unheard.

My fellow passengers and I
average together less than one
of this dwindling species of whale.
The collective expression
of our faces equals that
of the man who discovered fire,
or poetry.
                 From the water,
like nouns emerging suddenly known
from the flux of an alien language,
the whales beseech us in metre,
blunt flesh rhymed with a faith in life
that in the fistulous human mind
lies obdurate and dense as stone.

*James Baker Hall*

## OUR FALL WAS INTO FORGETFULNESS

We see them only
when they surface
but what we see takes us
down: the great grey whales
in their instinct, the long
undulating dream of nature
from the Bering Sea south:
they rise up heavy for air:
their knuckled backs turning up
out of the brine like water wheels
three slow times before they dive:
the sun-etched arrows of their tails
unfolding momentarily against the sky,
slapping water into light: then gone,
down again into the sea deep
within us.

       There was a time
before our time. Our fall was
into forgetfulness. We too
are endangered.

*Mary Oliver*

## HUMPBACKS

There is, all around us,
this country
of original fire.

You know what I mean.

The sky, after all, stops at nothing, so something
    has to be holding
our bodies
in its rich and timeless stables or else
we would fly away.

                    *


Off Stellwagen
off the Cape,
the humpbacks rise. Carrying their tonnage
    of barnacles and joy
they leap through the water, they nuzzle back under it
like children
at play.

                    *


They sing, too.
And not for any reason
you can't imagine.

                    *


Three of them
rise to the surface near the bow of the boat,
then dive
deeply, their huge scarred flukes
tipped to the air.

We wait, not knowing
just where it will happen; suddenly
they smash through the surface, someone begins
shouting for joy and you realize
it is yourself as they surge
upward and you see for the first time
how huge they are, as they breach,
and dive, and breach again

through the shining blue flowers
of the split water and you see them
for some unbelievable
part of a moment against the sky —
like nothing you've ever imagined —
like the myth of the fifth morning galloping
out of darkness, pouring
heavenward, spinning; then

                    *


they crash back under those black silks
and we all fall back
together into that wet fire, you
know what I mean.

                    *


I know a captain who has seen them
playing with seaweed, swimming
through the green islands, tossing
the slippery branches into the air.

I know a whale that will come to the boat whenever
she can, and nudge it gently along the bow
with her long flipper.

I know several lives worth living.

                    *


Listen, whatever it is you try
to do with your life, nothing will ever dazzle you
like the dreams of your body,

its spirit
longing to fly while the dead-weight bones

toss their dark mane and hurry
back into the fields of glittering fire

where everything,
even the great whale,
throbs with song.

*Charlotte Alexander*

## FINDRINNY

*("the joy, the freedom of whales")*

Today (we know so much)
we are told
    the dolphins and the whales
    have a highly developed system
    of communicating
    (from which we can learn).

But first, move through the water
just for the water's sake —
my water, yours,
forgetting which is which.

        Drift. Spin.
        Rise to our surface
        and dive again.

The water is a sacred place.
From it we come,
to recede, to return,
in daily unseen tides
like waves the whales ride on.

Your fingers, tongue touch
the outer bridges
of my heart's inner space,
forming an island structure
of us:
at its center the whale's song is told,
as yet unfathomable
but known.

*Celia Gilbert*

## WHALES SING

Whales sing.
Learning this, oh,
Another time we
Would have said,
*Praise Him.*

Now, praise them,
Our milk brothers, hunted,
As we are hunted,
Makers of songs,
A dying race.

They fashion for the few
Who lie, vast
And distant, listening
For one another,
A music, complex

Exalted. Their hoots
And echoes sound
The deepest registers
Of loneliness,
And love:
A *vox humana*
On the ocean's
Windy reed.

*John Frederick Nims*

## TIDE TURNING

Through salt marsh, grassy channel where the shark's
A rumor — lean, alongside — rides our boat;
Four of us off with picnic-things and wine.
Past tufty clutters of the mud called *pluff,*
Sun on the ocean tingles like a kiss.
About the fourth hour of the falling tide.

The six-hour-falling, six-hour-rising tide
Turns heron-haunts to alleys for the shark.
Tide-waters kiss and loosen; loosen, kiss.
Black-hooded terns blurt kazoo-talk — our boat
Now in midchannel and now rounding pluff.
Lolling, we eye the mud-tufts. Eye the wine.

The Atlantic, off there, dazzles. Who said wine-
Dark sea? Not this sea. Not at noon. The tide
Runs gold as chablis over sumps of pluff.
Too shallow here for lurkings of the shark,
His nose-cone, grin unsmiling. *Cr-ush!* the boat
Shocks, shudders — grounded. An abrupt tough kiss.

Our outboard's dug a mud-trough. Call that *kiss?*
Bronze knee bruised. A fair ankle gashed. With "wine-
Dark blood" a bard's on target here. The boat
Swivels, propeller in a pit, as tide
Withdraws in puddles round us — shows the shark-
Grey fin, grey flank, grey broadening humps of pluff.

Fingers that trailed in water, fume in pluff.
Wrist-deep, they learn how octopuses kiss.
Then — shark fins? No. Three dolphins there — *shh!* — arc
Coquettish. As on TV. Cup of wine
To you, slaphappy sidekicks! with the tide's
Last hour a mudflat draining round the boat.

The hourglass turns. Look, tricklings toward the boat.
The first hour, poky, picks away at pluff.
The second, though, swirls currents. Then the tide's
Third, fourth — abundance! the great ocean's kiss.
The last two slacken. So? We're free, for wine
And gaudier mathematics. Toast the shark,

Good shark, a no-show. Glory floats our boat.
We, with the wine remaining — done with pluff —
Carouse on the affluent kisses of the tide.

*William Pitt Root*

## REMEMBERING THE SEA ELEPHANT

Perhaps it is time for Candor,
with its big beak and clubbed feet,
to start its dance of extinction
toward the Smithsonian now,

while a few living members
of its race are still abroad
— the Gaffe, the Blunder, the Booboo,
the Inoperative Statement,

the Unauthorized Leak,
the Regrettable Figure of Speech —
while we can still tell one
when we meet it out and about.

Remember the Sea Elephant
at the turn of the century?
Only nine could be found
by the Smithsonian expedition,

which stuffed seven for us. Oh,
two were let go; perhaps
the crew was weary or orders
simply read seven. That pair

coupled relentlessly, for company.
Now, how they flourish at the edge
of our continent! So let us
send out our crew to snare Candor

for the permanent archives, leaving
a couple of Unguarded Remarks
at large, to do what they've
always done at the edge

of the continent of Lies
and Diplomacy — frisking openly,
enjoying the rocking waters,
nurturing the oddness

of their miraculous persistance,
preserving it for those of us
who may happen eventually
to the edge where we wonder

at the mewing and roaring,
the grumbling and cooing
in ourselves echoing
out there, loud and sure,

where prudent stone
is milled by careless surf
into the stuff we stand on
if we are to stand.

*Ann Mock-Bunting*

## THE TURTLE LADY

"I am watching fifteen nests now," the turtle lady said,
"five are between that dune and those sea oats.
Three should hatch late this week or early next."
We stood with waves breaking on our legs.
"Many people helped me with my first batch this year.
I raked a wide runway from the nest to the water
and placed a flashlight at the ocean.
Those babies think flashlights are the moon to follow.
While we waited the young people filled the crab holes with sand
and the seagulls and the pelicans flew above us.
For two hours the ground above the nest worked and moved
but it was as if suddenly a secret signal was given
when all at once those baby turtles bubbled to the surface
and headed straight for the sea.
I kept saying, 'This one is yours' and 'You take this one,'
assigning a person to watch each turtle,
making sure each baby was safe.
We waved the birds away, especially the gulls,
and pushed back any crabs
and every one of those turtles made it.
We counted close to two hundred."
She reached down and touched the sea with her fingers.
"You read about those things or see them on T.V.
but there's nothing until you see that ground work
right near your own feet."

*Colette Inez*

## SEA TURTLE

Writing news of her nest to foragers,
the sea turtle plows a path back to the
sea, and her sigh like a distant tide
lightly quakes in shoals of jelly fish,
among bristles and lacy stalks of plants.
When her hatchlings arrive, some to disappear
in foggy reefs, forests of rock and grass,
and at the end of a lost year, others to rise
and repeat their mother's ritual of slowly
gaining ground, she makes no sign of knowing
them. Like her, they will turn their backs
to the coast at night, probing the same road
to hollow out a ditch for the newborn,
blind sailors who will steer a course
to a landfall never seen, battering a trail
upwards toward the sun and outward
to the sea.

*Dallas Wiebe*

## ECOLOGY

Sea otters backstroke away
  from sliding cliffs.
They stare back
  at the falling island.
The golden eagle leans
  on the winds.
He sees the whirring blades
  of the cocked helicopter.
After all,
  a whale rolls
  up for air.
And the wolf howls
        sometimes.

Man thinks
  he owns the air.
Man thinks
  he owns the seas.
Man thinks he owns
      the woods.

The termites have something
  to say about that.
I hear them talking at night.
They say,
      "Soon he will not own
        his house."

*Philip Appleman*

## "SEA OTTER SURVIVAL ASSURED"

*The Fish and Game Department reports 591 otters*
*in the current census, 94 higher than last year.*

A million years before Darwin
this weasel slid into the sea
to tear at the brooding oysters
and roll wet eyes for the gliding
shadows of dim sea-monsters.
For a million years of birth
in the brine of the North Pacific
the fair exchange was fur
like ermine. When the big boats came,
bearing the hairless hunters,
the fittest betrayed his survival;
his skin was worth more than his life.

In a fog, five hundred otters
are nudging their young along
the coastline of California,
while monstrous in bed, the Pacific
is breaking with billions of faces,
turbaned men from the Punjab,
brown-eyed girls with rice bowls,
horsemen waving their rifles —
and five hundred otters thrashing
the bell of a bedside alarm.

*Survival assured:* across
the pacific waves of blanket
someone as blond as hope
speaks from the edges of sleeping:
"Morning is out there again,
on the other side of the curtains."

Natural Selection,
we have come through another night,
come to one more day.

*Lennart Bruce*

## THE WOUNDED OCEAN

is striking out:
it started to rain,
but indoors, some kind of tears
or sweat. The swallows
left long ago   Crabs and other

rats of the sea appear indoors,
climb the highrises for the sky
People leave their jobs, flee
office buildings and homes, drift
in the sun drying clothes,
soothing limbs aching from cold.

The rust eats machines, factories,
warehouses. Plumbers work around the
clock. Drownings increase   Nobody knows
how to stop the indoor rains   Instruments
won't function in the rot   Research
dissolves, findings float away

The waterproof houses fill up and burst
like overgrown drops. "Bankruptcy"
assumes its true meaning: ruptured banks
Stock, real estate, values dissolve
The only art that prevails is tattoo,
all else is washed away

The deluge comes down in church,
in the theater, City Hall, the UN, in jail,
the hospitals: the rain splashes the wounds
between the hands of the surgeons
Ancient rain songs are reversed and sung
by congregations soaked to their bones

Praying monks wander about under umbrellas
in their cells. Cities sink, sewers' stench
is washed away   Fireflies glow in the marshes
Cemeteries are flooded, caskets and bones
surface in their swamps   The living point at
them and say: "The dead have risen"

*Deena Metzger*

## *from* ENDANGERED SPECIES

If it were only a question of whales   or
only of Indians   if it were only a question of women   if
it were only half the creatures of the world   who needed
saving   perhaps we could put out our arms   if only something;
would act against this increase   if all that multiplication
would diminish   if it were only milk at my breast   and
not cancer   if it were only a child in the womb   and
not cancer   if the wild growth   were geranium and morning
glory   if it were not lovers sliding from us   like dead
skins   if it were not the multiplication of losses   if
we could find one place to make a stand   if the entire world
were not in danger   if we could stop now   this instant
as we're walking   and watch the ocean leap up at us   and
return constant   we could probably put out our hands   but
there are more in them than whales   more in them than women
more threatened by extinction than we can encompass

We put out our hands   but we can not close the circle
so we walk on the beach   begging the night   to hide the
creatures we love   we walk on the beach   our hands at
our sides   thousands of miles between us   the whales
calling from the sea.

## OCEAN

The gray whales are going south: I see their fountains
Rise from black sea: great dark bulks of hot blood
Plowing the deep cold sea to their trysting-place
Off Mexican California, where water is warm, and love
Finds massive joy: from the flukes to the blowhole the whole giant
Flames like a star. In February storm the ocean
Is black and rainbowed; the high spouts of white spray
Rise and fall over in the wind. There is no April in the ocean;
How do these creatures know that spring is at hand?
  They remember their ancestors
That crawled on earth: the little fellows like otters, who took to sea
And have grown great. Go out to the ocean, little ones,
You will grow great or die.


      And there the small trout
Flicker in the streams that tumble from the coast mountain,
Little quick flames of life: but from time to time
One of them goes mad, wanting room and freedom; he slips
         between the rock jaws
And takes to sea, where from time immemorial
The long sharks wait. If he lives he becomes a steelhead,
A rainbow trout grown beyond nature in the ocean. Go out to the
           great ocean,
Grow great or die.

     O ambitious children,
It would be wiser no doubt to rest in the brook
And remain little. But if the devil drives
I hope you will scull far out to the wide ocean and find your fortune
         and beware of teeth.

It is not important. There are deeps you will never reach and peaks
        you will never explore,
Where the great squids and kraken lie in the gates, in the awful
         twilight
The whip-armed hungers; and mile under mile below,
Deep under deep, on the deep floor, in the darkness
Under the weight of the world: like lighted galleons the ghost-fish,
With phosphorescent portholes along their flanks,
Sail over and eat other: the condition of life,
To eat each other: but in the slime below
Prodigious worms as great and as slow as glaciers burrow in the
         sediment,

Mindless and blind, huge tubes of muddy flesh
Sucking not meat but carrion, drippings and offal
From the upper sea. They move a yard in a year,
Where there are no years, no sun, no season, darkness and slime;
They spend nothing on action, all on gross flesh.

                                                O ambitious ones,
Will you grow great, or die? It hardly matters; the words are
                                                comparative;
Greatness is but less little; and death's changed life.

*Richard Wilbur*

## ADVICE TO A PROPHET

When you come, as you soon must, to the streets of our city,
Mad-eyed from stating the obvious,
Not proclaiming our fall but begging us
In God's name to have self-pity,

Spare us all word of the weapons, their force and range,
The long numbers that rocket the mind;
Our slow, unreckoning hearts will be left behind,
Unable to fear what is too strange.

Nor shall you scare us with talk of the death of the race.
How should we dream of this place without us? —
The sun mere fire, the leaves untroubled about us,
A stone look on the stone's face?

Speak of the world's own change. Though we cannot conceive
Of an undreamt thing, we know to our cost
How the dreamt cloud crumbles, the vines are blackened by frost,
How the view alters. We could believe,

If you told us so, that the white-tailed deer will slip
Into perfect shade, grown perfectly shy,
The lark avoid the reaches of our eye,
The jack-pine lose its knuckled grip

On the cold ledge, and every torrent burn
As Xanthus once, its gliding trout
Stunned in a twinkling. What should we be without
The dolphin's arc, the dove's return,

These things in which we have seen ourselves and spoken?
Ask us, prophet, how we shall call
Our natures forth when that live tongue is all
Dispelled, that glass obscured or broken

In which we have said the rose of our love and the clean
Horse of our courage, in which beheld
The singing locust of the soul unshelled,
And all we mean or wish to mean.

Ask us, ask us whether with the worldless rose
Our hearts shall fail us; come demanding
Whether there shall be lofty or long standing
When the bronze annals of the oak-tree close.

**Aelbert Aehegma** is a multi-media artist whose books include *No Poems, The Big Island,* and translations of Hawaiian creation myths. (Hawaii)

**Charlotte Alexander** edits *Outerbridge* and has published works in *Carleton Miscellany, Prairie Schooner, Greenfield Review, Arts in Society, Poet Lore* and *Mid-American Review.* (New York)

**Philip Appleman**'s books include *Darwin's Ark, Apes and Angels, Shame the Devil, Kites on a Windy Day, Summer Love and Surf, Open Doorways,* two novels and several works of non-fiction. (New York)

**Michael Benedikt's** fifth collection of poetry is *The Badminton at Great Barrington, or Gustav Mahler and The Chattanooga Choo-Choo.* He has edited a number of anthologies of European and American drama and poetry, among them *The Prose Poem: An International Anthology* and *The Poetry of Surrealism.* His own work appears in some 45 anthologies. (New York)

**Carol Berge**, who has edited *Center Magazine* and *Mississippi Review,* has published twenty books, including *Couple Called Moebius, Acts of Love,* and *Fierce Metronome.* (New Mexico)

**James Bertolino**'s books include *Broken Spring, First Credo, Precinct Kali and The Gertrude Spicer Story, No Black Sticks, New and Selected Poems.* He is currently editing an anthology of potato poems. (Washington)

**Linda Bierds**' books include *Flights of the Harvest Mare, Off the Aleutian Chain,* and *Snaring the Flightless Birds: the Legends of Maui.* She has poems in *New Letters, New England Review, Massachusetts Review,* and *Hudson Review.* (Washington)

**Robert Bly**'s many books of poetry, prose and translation include *The Man in the Black Coat Returns, The Morning Glory,* and *Times Alone: Selected Poems of Antonio Machado,* translated from Spanish. His work is the subject of a recent collection of essays, *Robert Bly: When Sleepers Awake.* (Minnesota)

**Paula Bonnell** is an attorney, whose poetry has been published in *Southern Poetry Review, MS., Christian Science Monitor, New York Times Book Review, Boston Review,* and others. She is a PEN Syndicated Fiction Award winner. (Massachusetts)

**Kay Boyle**'s thirty-seven books include *This Is Not a Letter, Words That Must Be Said: Selected Poems of Kay Boyle 1927-1984, Testament for My Students, Collected Poems, A Glad Day, Primer for Combat, Monday Night, Death of a Man, My Next Bride, Gentleman, I Address You Privately, Year Before Last, Plagued by the Nightingale,* and *The Smoking Mountain.* (Oregon)

**Alan Britt**'s books include *The Afternoon of the Light,* and *Last Tango in Baltimore.* (Maryland)

**Lennart Bruce** has published eleven books, including *A True Saga* (autobiography in Swedish), *Letters of Credit, Subpoams,* and *The Broker.* (California)

**Joseph Bruchac** has published more than twenty books, including *Near The Mountain, Survival This Way, Keepers of the Earth, Remembering the Dawn,* and *No Telephone to Heaven.* He is editor of *The Greenfield Review* and the anthologies *Songs From This Earth on Turtle's Back,* and *Breaking Silence: an Anthology of Contemporary Asian-American Poets.* (New York)

**Siv Cedering**'s books include *Mother Is, Letters From The Floating World, The Blue Horse,* two novels, and books for children in both English and Swedish. (New York)

**Maxine Combs**, winner of the 1988 Larry Neal Fiction Award, is the author of *Swimming Out of the Collective Unconscious* (poetry), *Handbook of the Strange* (novel) and *The Foam of Perilous Seas* (stories). (District of Columbia)

**Sarah Cotterill**, author of *The Hive Burning,* has poems in *American Poetry Review, Ploughshares, Carolina Quarterly, Nimrod, Poetry Now* and *Webster Review.* (Maryland)

**Philip Dacey**'s work includes *The Man With Red Suspenders, Fives, Gerard Manley Hopkins Meets Walt Whitman in Heaven and Other Poems,* and *The Boy Under the Bed.* (Minnesota)

**Ann Darr**, a pilot in the Women's Airforce Services during World War II, has published five collections: *St. Ann's Gut, The Myth of a Woman's Fist, Cleared for Landing, Riding With the Fireworks,* and *Do You Take This Woman.* She won a Discovery Award from The Poetry Center in New York. (Maryland)

**David B. de Leeuw**'s first collection of poems is *I Could See The Rainbow on My Pillow.* (New Jersey)

**Diana Der Hovanessian**'s books include *How To Choose Your Past, For You On New Year's Day, Land of Fire,* and *Come Sit Beside Me and Listen to Koutchag,* translations of Armenian writers. (Massachusetts)

**William Doreski**'s books include *Earth That Sings, The Testament of Israel Potter,* and *Half of the Map.* (New Hampshire)

**Alan Dugan** lives on Cape Cod. His many books include *New and Collected Poems: 1961-1983.* (Massachusetts)

**Stephen Dunn**'s collections of poems include *Not Dancing, A Circus of Whales* and *Work and Love.* (New Jersey)

**Stuart Dybeck**'s poetry and fiction includes *The Two Deaths of Senora Puccini, Brass Knuckles* and *Childhood and Other Neighborhoods.* (Michigan)

**W. D. Ehrhart** has edited collections of work by Vietnam veterans. His books include *Winter Bells, Vietnam-Perkasie, To Those Who Have Gone Home Tired, The Samisdat Poems, The Outer Banks, Matters of the Heart,* and *The Awkward Silence.* (Pennsylvania)

**Donald Finkel**'s books include *The Wake of the Electron, Selected Shorter Poems, The Garbage Wars, What Manner of Beast, The Detachable Man* and *Endurance and Going Under.* (Missouri)

**Brenden Galvin**'s books include *Winter Oysters, Atlantic Flyway, A Birder's Dozen,* and *Seals in the Inner Harbor.* (Connecticut)

**Brewster Ghiselin**'s most recent book is *Windrose: Poems 1929-1979.* (Utah)

**Robert Gibbs**'s books include *Whalesongs, Momentary Days, The Margins, The Winter House,* and *The Names of Earth in Summer.* His *A Geography of Common Names* won the 1987 Devil's Millhopper Press Award. (Pennsylvania)

**Celia Gilbert**, the author of *Bonfire, Queen of Darkness* and the long poem, ''Lot's Wife,'' has won a Discovery Award. (Massachusetts)

**Albert Goldbarth**'s twelve books of poems include *Arts and Sciences, Comings Back* and *Original Light: New and Selected Poems.* (Texas, Kansas)

**Jan Goodloe**'s poetry has appeared in *Yellow Silk* and *Studia Mystica.* (California)

**Art Goodtime**'s books include *Embracing the Earth, Sparks of Fire, Kehoe Beach,* and *Dancing on the Brink of the World.* He edits *Wolverine* and *Earth First.* (Colorado)

**Michael Gregory**'s books include *Hunger Weather, The Valley Floor, Song of the Beast* (with Charles Dietz) and *What's in the Smoke: A Breather's Guide to Douglas Smelter Pollution.* (Arizona)

**James Baker Hall**'s books include *Stopping On The Edge To Wave, The Short Hall,* and *Getting It On Up to the Brag.* His work appears in *The New Yorker, Ploughshares,* and *Poetry.* (Kentucky)

The late **Jack Hand**'s poetry appeared in *Yarrow, American Weave, The Missouri Poet, Cumberland Poetry Review,* and *Missouri Review* and is collected in *At The End of the World Bazaar.* (Missouri)

**Richard Harteis** is former director of the PEN Syndicated Fiction Project. His work includes *Marathon, Fourteen Women,* and *Moroccan Journal,* as well as short fiction and theater pieces. (Maryland)

**Penny Harter**'s books include *The Price of Admission, The Monkey's Face, In The Broken Curve, White Flowers in the Snow, Hiking the Crevasse,* and *Lovepoems.* She won the Poetry Society of America's 1987 Davis Award. (New Jersey)

**Judith Hemschemeyer**'s books include *I Remember, The Room Was Filled With Light, Very Close and Very Slow,* and a three-volume translation of Anna Akhmatova's poems. (New York)

The late **Raymond Henri**, a Marine Corps colonel, published four books on Marine Corps activities in addition to his book of poems, *Dispatches From the Fields.* (New York)

**Daniel Hoffman** served as Poetry Consultant at the Library of Congress. His books include *Hang-Gliding from Helicon: New and Selected Poems, 1948-1988, Brotherly Love, An Armada of Thirty Whales, Broken Laws,* and *The Center of Attention.* (Pennsylvania)

The late **Barbara A. Holland**'s books include *Running Backwards, Autumn Numbers,* and *In the Shadows.* (New York)

**Colette Inez**'s books include *Family Life, Eight Minutes From the Sun, Alive and Taking Names,* and *The Woman Who Loved Worms,* which won the 1972 Great Lake Colleges' Association Award. (New York)

**William Inman** has taught in prisons, worked with the mentally handicapped, and edited *New Kauri.* His books include *A Way Through for the Damned* and *A Trek of Waiting.* (Arizona)

**Robinson Jeffers** (1887-1962) was born in Pittsburgh, but spent most of his life in Carmel, on the California coast. His books include *The Double Axe, Hungerfield, The Beginning and the End,* and *The Selected Poetry of Robinson Jeffers.* His translation of *Medea* (1946) was performed on Broadway. (California)

**Beth Joselow**, literary editor of *Washington Review,* has published in *The New Yorker, Primavera,* and *American Poetry Review.* Her books include *April Wars, Gypsies,* and *Ice Fishing,* (District of Columbia)

**Nancy Roxbury Knutson**'s collection of poems *Nothing Should Fall to Waste* won the Artist's Wreath Award. Her work has appeared in *Nimrod* and *American Poetry Review.* (Florida)

**Ernest Kroll**, a former newspaperman and U.S. government official, has published five books, including *Tattoo Parlor and Other Poems* and *50 Fraxioms.* (District of Columbia)

**Donald Kummings**' poetry has appeared in *The Spoon River Quarterly, Poetry Now,* and other journals. He is the author of *Walt Whitman, 1940-1975: A Reference Guide.* (Wisconsin)

**Stanley Kunitz**, a former Consultant in Poetry at the Library of Congress, has received numerous awards and honors for his work, including the Pulitzer Prize. He was editor of the Yale Series of Younger Poets. Among his many books of poems and translations are *The Wellfleet Whale and Companion Poems, A Kind of Order, A Kind of Folly: Essays and Conversations, The Poems of Stanley Kunitz, 1928-1978,* and, most recently, *Next-to-Last Things: A Miscellany.* (New York)

**Naomi Lazard**'s poetry has appeared in *The New Yorker, Translation, The Nation,* and *Poet Lore.* She translated *The True Subject.* (New York)

**Virginia Linton** won the 1972 Guinness Award for "With Differing Views of a Dead Whale" from her book, *Heading Out.* The late poet's work appeared in *The London Daily Telegraph Magazine, The Poetry Society of America Bulletin,* and *South Carolina Review.* (South Carolina)

**Duane Locke** has published eleven books of poetry, including *Foam on Gulf Shore, From The Bottom of the Sea, Inland Oceans, Dead Cities, Submerged Ferns, Light Bulbs,* and *Lengthened Eyelashes.* (Florida)

**Clarinda Harriss Lott**, founder and editor of The New Poets Series in Baltimore, wrote *The Bone Tree,* and is co-author of *Forms of Verse: British and American.* (Maryland)

**Morton Marcus**' books of poetry include *Pages From a Scrapbook of Immigrants, Big Winds, Glass Mornings,* and *Shadows Cast by Stars: Poems 1972-1980.* (California)

**Linda McCarriston**'s book *Talking Soft Dutch* was a finalist in the AWP award series. She won the 1983 Grolier Prize and has published in *Poetry, Ploughshares,* and other magazines. (Vermont)

**Peter Meinke's** collections of poems include *Night Watch on the Chesapeake, Trying to Surprise God, The Rat Poems, The Night Train and The Golden Bird,* and *Lines from Neuchatel.* His story collection, *The Piano Tuner,* won the 1986 Flannery O'Connor Award. (Florida)

**Deena Metzger** collaborated on a documentary film, "Chile: With Poems and Guns." Her six books include *Skin, Shadows/Silence,* and *The Book of Hags.* (California)

**Arthur McA. Miller** is co-editor of *New CollAge Magazine.* His poems have appeared in *Beloit Poetry Journal, Tendril, Gryphon,* and *Stone Country.* (Florida)

**Ann Mock-Bunting**'s work has appeared in *North American Review, Iowa Woman, The Arts Journal* and others. (Florida)

**Judith Moffett**'s books include *Keeping Time, Whinny Moor Crossing,* and a critical study, *James Merrill: An Introduction to the Poetry.* (Pennsylvania)

**Patricia Monaghan**, a lifelong Alaskan, recently moved to Chicago, where she is a poetry reviewer for *Booklist* and teaches in a literacy program. Her books are *Winterburning* (poems) and *The Book of Goddesses and Heroines.* (Alaska, Illinois)

**Frederick Morgan** is editor of *Hudson Review.* His books include *Poems: New and Selected, Northbrook, Poems of the Two Worlds, Eleven Poems, Seven Poems by Mallarmé, Refractions, Death Mother and Other Poems.* (New York)

**Howard Nelson** is author of *Creatures* and *Robert Bly: An Introduction to the Poetry.* (New York)

**Mariah Burton Nelson's** forthcoming book is *Passion Plays: When Women Athletes Compete for Love or Money.* She is contributing editor of several sports magazines and a *Washington Post* columnist. (California, Virginia)

**Pablo Neruda** (1904-1973), the eminent Chilean poet and diplomat, won the Nobel Prize for Literature in 1971. (Chile)

**Shelia Nickerson**, poet and artist, edits *Alaska Fish and Game.* Some of her books include *In the Compass of Unrest, Feast of the Animals, An Alaska Bestiary,* and *Songs of the Pine Wife.* (Alaska)

**John Frederick Nims**, a former editor of *Poetry*, edited the 1987 *Norton Book of Verse.* Some of his many books include *The Kiss: A Jambalaya, Selected Poems,* and *A Local Habitation*, a collection of essays on poetry. (Illinois)

**Kathryn Nocerino's** books include *Death of the Plankton Bar and Grill, Head with Hat, Candles in the Daytime,* and *Waxhips.* (New York)

**Julia Older** has published eight books, both poetry and non-fiction, including *A Little Wild, Oonts and Others, Appalachian Odyssey, Endometriosis,* and *Cooking Without Fuel.* Her work has appeared in *The New Yorker, Literary Review,* and others. (New Hampshire)

**Mary Oliver** lives in Provincetown. She received a Pulitzer Prize in 1983 for *American Primitive.* Her other collections of poems include *Twelve Moons, The River Styx, Ohio and Other Poems,* and *No Voyages and Other Poems,* and two chapbooks. Her work appears in many magazines and literary publications, including *The New Yorker, The Atlantic, Harvard Magazine,* and *Yankee.* (Massachusetts)

**Fredda S. Pearlson**'s work has appeared in *California Quarterly, Helicon Nine, The Centennial Review,* and other magazines. She is an advertising/marketing writer and consultant. (New York)

**Edmund Pennant's** books of poems include *I, Too, Jehovah, Dream's Navel,* and *Misapprehension and Other Poems.* He has been awarded the Poetry Society of America's Alfred Kreymborg and Mary Carolyn Davies Prizes. (New York)

**Simon Perchik** has written ten books including *The Club Fits Either Hand, Gandolf Poems, The Snowcat Poems,* and *Mr. Lucky.* His poems have appeared in *Poetry, Harvard Magazine,* and many others. (New York)

**Geoff Peterson**, formerly editor of *Willow Spring*, has had work in *Maelstrom Review, High Rock Review, Topo,* and others. (North Carolina)

**Roger Pfingston's** books of poems and stories include *Something Iridescent* and *The Circus of Unreasonable Acts.* He was a PEN Syndicated Fiction winner. (Indiana)

**Marge Piercy** has written eleven books of poetry and nine novels, including: *My Mother's Body; Gone To Soldiers; Fly Away Home; The Moon is Always Female; Stone, Paper, Knife;* and *Available Light.* (Massachusetts)

**Kenneth Pobo's** books include *Billions of Lit Cigarettes, Evergreen*, and *A Pause Inside Dusk*. His work has appeared in *Tendril, Poetry Now, Indiana Review*, and others. (Pennsylvania)

**Al Poulin, Jr.'s** books include *A Momentary Order, Makers and Lovers, Begin Again*, and *Migration of Powers*. He has translated four volumes of Rilke's French poems. (New York)

**James Ragan's** works include *In the Talking Hours* and two plays: *Saints* and *The Gandy Dancers*. His work has appeared in *Ohio Review, Denver Quarterly*, and others. (California)

**David Ray**, a former editor of *New Letters* and several anthologies, won the 1979 William Carlos Williams Award for *The Tramp's Cup*. His numerous other books include *Sam's Book, That Maharan's New Wall, Encounter at Shaky Bridge*, and others. Several of his stories were PEN Syndicated Fiction Project winners. (Missouri)

**Carlos Reyes**, translator of Pablo Neruda's poems, has published several books including *Nightmarks: New and Selected Poems, The Shingle Weaver's Journal*, and *At Doolin Quay*. (Oregon)

**William Pitt Root's** publications include three books of poems, *Invisible Guests, Reasons For Going It On Foot*, and *Fault Dancing*. He won *Southern Poetry Review's* Guy Owen Prize. (New York)

**Norman Rosten** is a poet and novelist whose recent books include *Love in All Its Disguises, Neighborhood Tales, Marilyn Among Friends*, and *Selected Poems*. (New York)

**May Sarton's** forty-third book, *The Silence Now: New and Uncollected Earlier Poems*, follows *At Seventy: A Journal*. She has published poetry, novels, journals and other nonfiction, and books for children. Her other poetry collections include *Letters From Maine: New Poems, Halfway To Silence*, and *Collected Poems, 1930-1973*. (Maine)

**Marnette Saz's** articles and poems have been widely published in the feminist press throughout New England. (Massachusetts)

**Hillel Schwartz's** books include *Century's End* (forthcoming), *Phantom Children*, and *Never Satisfied*, a history of dieting. He won the 1988 Richard Hugo Prize from *Poetry Northwest*, and his poetry and fiction have appeared in many publications. (California)

**Michael Shorb** has written extensively about endangered species and other environmental concerns. His essays and poems have appeared in the *Nation, Michigan Quarterly, Poetry Now*, and other publications. (California)

**Robert Siegel's** books include *Whalesong, The Kingdom of Wundle, In A Pig's Eye*, and *The Wyrm of Grog*. His work has appeared in *The New Yorker, Poetry*, and the *Atlantic*. (Wisconsin)

**Atanas Slavov** published science fiction, poetry and ethnography in Bulgaria before defecting to the USA. His books in English are *The Thaw in Bulgarian Literature, Mr. Lampedusa Has Vanished* (poetry), and *With The Precision of Bats*, a non-fiction novel. (Maryland)

**William Stafford**, former Consultant in Poetry at the Library of Congress, has won numerous honors and awards for his poetry, including the National Book Award. Some of his many books are *An Oregon Message, You Must Revise Your Life, A Glass Face in The Rain, Writing the Australian Crawl*, and *Stories That Could Be True: New and Collected Poems*. (Oregon)

**Ann Stanford's** books include *In Mediterranean Air, Dreaming The Garden*, and *Anne Bradstreet: The Worldly Puritan*. The late poet received awards from the National Institute of the Academy of Arts and Letters and the Poetry Society of America. (California)

**Margo Stever's** poetry has been published in *Ironwood, Poetry Now, New England Review*, and other journals. She runs the Sleepy Hollow Poetry Series in Tarrytown. (New York)

**D.E. Steward**, an ex-forester, has published one novel, *Contact Inhibition*, and *Four Stories*. His work has appeared in *Carolina Quarterly* and *Gargoyle*, among others. (New Jersey)

**Brian Swann**, poetry editor of *Amicus*, is author of five books of poetry, including *The Middle of the Journey*; five books of short fiction, including *The Plot of the Mice*; three books for children; and sixteen volumes of translations. (New York)

**John Tagliabue's** books include *Poems, A Japanese Journal, The Buddha Uproar, The Doorless Door, The Great Day,* and *Asian Notebooks.* (Maine)

**Nathaniel Tarn's** books include *Atilan/Alaska, Lyrics for the Bride of God,* and *At the Western Gates.* (New Mexico)

**Madeline Tiger's** books include *Keeping House in This Forest, Toward Spring Bank,* and *Electric Blanket.* Her work has appeared in *American Poetry Review* and *The Literary Review.* (New Jersey)

**Lewis Turco's** books include *A Maze of Monsters, American Still Lifes, The Book of Forms, Pocoangelini: A Fantography and Other Poems* and *The Compleat Melancholick.* (New York)

**Constance Urdang** has published three collections of poetry: *Lucha, Only the World, The Lone Woman and Others,* and a novella, *American Earthquakes.* (Missouri)

**Ellen Bryant Voigt's** books include *Claiming Kin* and *The Forces of Plenty.* Her poems have appeared in *The New Yorker, The Atlantic, The Nation,* and *Antaeus.* (Vermont)

**Jeanne Voege** is a freelance journalist, naturalist and poetry editor of *Artsnews.* Her collections of poems include *New Wave Sex* and *Risings.* (New York)

**Dorothy Ward** has published in numerous literary magazines, including *Intro 8, Travois, Texas Portfolio,* and *Bloomsbury Review.* (Texas)

**Margaret Weaver** has published poems in *Yankee, Visions, Poet Lore, Kyriokos, Kavitha, Taurus,* and other magazines. (Maryland)

**Sarah Brown Weitzman's** poetry has appeared in *Tendril, Poetry Now, The Manhattan Poetry Review,, Bellingham Review, Southwestern Review,* and others. (New York)

**Dallas Wiebe** edits *Cincinnati Poetry Review* and *Black Ice.* His works of fiction include *Transparent Eye-Ball* and *Skyblue The Badass.* He has published in *Paris Review, Fiction International,* and other magazines. (Ohio)

**Richard Wilbur**, a former Poet Laureate and Poetry Consultant at the Library of Congress, has won the Pulitzer, Bollinger, Prix de Rome, and many other awards for his poetry, drama and translations from the French and Russian. His books include *The Poems of Richard Wilbur, Walking to Sleep, Advice to A Prophet, Things of This World, Ceremony, The Beautiful Changes* and a book "for children and others" called *Opposites.* (Massachusetts)

**Peter Wild's** books include *The Afternoon in Dismay, Wilderness,* and *Cochise.* His poems are widely published. (Arizona)

**Edward P. Willey** has published in many journals, including *Light Year, Midway Review, Vanderbilt Review,* and *Poetry Now.* (South Carolina)

**Adrienne Wolfert's** books include *Natal Fire, Sewing the Duck,* and *Discovery of the Human Fossil.* Her poems have appeared in *Louisville Review, Poetry Review, North American Review,* and *Confrontation.* (Connecticut)

---

**Elisavietta Ritchie**, editor of *The Dolphin's Arc*, has seven collections of poetry, including *Tightening The Circle Over Eel Country* (winner of the Great Lakes Colleges Association Award), and *Raking The Snow.* Three of her stories have been PEN Syndicated Fiction Award winners. She translates Russian and French and edits art catalogues. (District of Columbia)

**Julia S. Child** is a biological illustrator whose drawings appear in textbooks, including Claude Zillee's *Biology,* and in professional journals. For the past 14 years, she has taught biological drawing at The Children's School of Science in Woods Hole, Massachusetts. (Connecticut)

**David Doubilet's** photographs frequently appear in National Geographic Society publications, including *Dolphins: Our Friends in the Sea* by Judith E. Rinard. (New York)

The editor thanks the poets and publishers who donated their poems to this project. Unless otherwise stated, the copyright is held by the author. All poems are used by permission.

**Aelbert Aehegma,** "Ancient Turtle Dance," from TURTLE DANCE: *Poems of Hawaii and Translations of the Polynesian Creation Chant, "The Kumulipo"* by Aelbert Aehegma, Oceanic Publishing Co., copyright ©1984 by Aelbert Aehegma, first appeared in *Ka Huliau.* **Charlotte Alexander,** "Findrinny," first appeared in *The Carleton Miscellany,* Jan. 1975, Vol. XV, #1. **Philip Appleman,** "Sea Otter Survival Assured" from SUMMER LOVE AND SURF by Philip Appleman, Vanderbilt University Press, 1968. **Michael Benedikt,** "Of Seals, and Our Smiles" first appeared in *PSA Poetry Review,* 1982, Vol. 1, No. 1. **Carol Berg,** "Grey, or Turtle, Song," from FIERCE METRONOME: *The One-Page Novels* by Carol Berg, Window Press, 1981. **James Bertolino,** "Consider the Whales," from FIRST CREDO by James Bertolino, Quarterly Review of Literature Poetry Series, 1986. **Linda Bierds,** "Elegy for 41 Whales Beached in Florence, Oregon, June, 1979" from FLIGHTS OF THE HARVEST-MARE by Linda Bierds, Ahsahta Press, Boise State University, 1985, first appeared in *New Letters.* **Robert Bly,** "The Dead Seal Near McClure's Beach," from THE MORNING GLORY: *Prose Poems* by Robert Bly, copyright ©1975 by Robert Bly, (Harper & Row) first appeared in *Choice.* Reprinted with permission of the author. **Paula Bonnell,** "They Are Right; They are Aware; Their Awareness Is Rightness, But They Are Not Aware Of That" first appeared in *Aspect,* No. 58, Sept.–Oct., 1974. **Kay Boyle,** "Reincarnation" from THIS IS NOT A LETTER by Kay Boyle, Sun and Moon Press, 1985, copyright ©1983 by Kay Boyle. **Alan Britt,** "The Baby Harp Seal," from THE AFTERNOON OF THE LIGHT by Alan Britt, University of Tampa Press, 1982. **Siv Cedering,** "Cetus, A Letter from Jonah," first appeared in *Poetry Now.* **Maxine Combs,** "February 11, 1983," from SWIMMING OUT OF THE COLLECTIVE UNCONSCIOUS, copyright ©1988 by Maxine Combs, The Wineberry Press; first appeared in FINDING THE NAME. **Sarah Cotterill,** "Harp Seals" first appeared in *Webster Review,* Vol. 9, No. 1, copyright ©1983 by Webster Review. Used by permission. **Philip Dacey,** "I Ask the Whale, Why?" from FISH SWEET GIRAFFE THE LION SNAKE AND OWL by Philip Dacey, Back Door Press, 1970. **Ann Darr,** "Hit It With the Baby," from THE MYTH OF A WOMAN'S FIST, copyright ©1973 by Ann Darr, (William Morrow & Co.). **Diana Der Hovanessian,** "Whale," reprinted by permission of The Christian Science Monitor Publishing Co., copyright ©1983. **Alan Dugan,** "Untitled Poem," ("One used to be able to say") copyright ©1961, 1962, 1968, 1972, 1973, 1974, 1983 by Alan Dugan. From NEW AND COLLECTED POEMS: *1961-1983* by Alan Dugan, published by The Ecco Press in 1983. Reprinted by permission. **Stephen Dunn,** "Having Lost all Capacity," from WORK AND LOVE by Stephen Dunn, Carnegie-Mellon University Press, 1981, first appeared in *The Ohio Review.* **Stuart Dybeck,** "Inside the Turtle," first appeared in *Bits.* **W. D. Ehrhart,** "The Death of Kings," first appeared in THE SAMISDAT POEMS by W. D. Ehrhart, Samisdat Press, 1980. **Donald Finkel,** "MMMMMM," from WHAT MANNER OF BEAST by Donald Finkel, copyright ©1981 by Atheneum Press. **Brendan Galvin,** "Seals in the Inner Harbor" from SEALS IN THE INNER HARBOR by Brendan Galvin, Carnegie-Mellon University Press, 1986, first appeared in *The New Republic,* copyright ©1982. Reprinted by permission of *The New Republic.* **Brewster Ghiselin,** "Orca," from WINDROSE: *Poems, 1929-1979* by Brewster Ghiselin, first appeared in *Concerning Poetry,* Spring 1969. Reprinted with permission of the author. **Robert Gibb,** "The Flensers," from WHALESONGS by Robert Gibb, Turkey Press, 1979. **Celia Gilbert,** "Whales Sing," from QUEEN OF DARKNESS by Celia Gilbert, copyright ©1972 by Celia Gilbert. All rights reserved. Printed by permission of Viking Penguin Inc. **Albert Goldbarth,** "Dolphin: Monologue and Song," from COMINGS BACK by Albert

editors. **Mary Oliver,** "Humpbacks" from American Primitive: *Poems by Mary Oliver,* copyright ©1983 by Mary Oliver, an Atlantic Monthly Press Book published by Little Brown and Company and used by permission of the publisher, first appeared in *Country Journal.* **Simon Perchik,** "*" ("The turtle once twins, the sea . . . ") from The Club Fits Either Hand by Simon Perchik, The Elizabeth Press. **Geoff Peterson,** "The Rapture" first appeared in *Visions.* **Roger Pfingston,** "The Newt and The Whale," from Something Iridescent by Roger Pfingston, Barnwood Press, 1987, first appeared in *Washout Review* and then in The Circus of Unreasonable Acts by Roger Pfingston, Year's Press, 1982. **Marge Piercy,** "Another Country" from The Moon Is Always Female by Marge Piercy, copyright ©1980 by Marge Piercy, by permission of Alfred A. Knopf, Inc. **A. Poulin, Jr.,** "Children in Fog," from A Momentary Order: Poems, copyright ©1987 by A. Poulin, Jr. Reprinted by permission of Graywolf Press, it first appeared in *New Letters.* **James Ragan,** "Backward Years," from In the Talking Hours by James Ragan, copyright ©1979. **David Ray,** "The Humpbacks," copyright ©1988 by David Ray. **Carlos Reyes,** "Aun XXIV" by Pablo Neruda from Aun (Yet Another Day), Copper Canyon Press, copyright ©1987, first appeared in *Bitter Oleander,* Vol. 2, No. 1 (1976) and is used by permission. **William Pitt Root,** "Remembering the Sea Elephant," first appeared in *Poetry,* August 1984, copyright ©1984, The Modern Poetry Association. Reprinted by permission of the editors of *Poetry.* **Norman Rosten,** "Baby Whale in Captivity," copyright ©1988 by Norman Rosten. **May Sarton,** "Who Knows Where the Joy Goes," from Letters from Maine by May Sarton. W.W. Norton, 1985. Used by permission. **Hillel Schwartz,** "On the Whales of the California Desert," first appeared in *Colorado State Review,* #8, 1, Fall/Winter, 1980. **Michael Shorb,** "Whale Walker's Morning," first appeared in *Michigan Quarterly Review.* **Atanas Slavov,** "Goliath," from P.S. Mr. Lampedusa Has Vanished, Occidental Press, 1982. **William Stafford,** "A Morning," first appeared in *Johns Hopkins Magazine.* **Margo Stever,** "Ascension," first appeared in *The Webster Review,* Vol. 8, No. 2, 1983. **Brian Swann,** "Pig Moon, Turtle Moon" first appeared in *Chicago Review.* **John Tagliabue,** "Smooth and Gleaming," first appeared in *The Greenfield Review,* 1985. **Nathaniel Tarn,** "Four Sections from Journal of the Laguna de San Ignacio," from At the Western Gates by Nathaniel Tarn, Tooth of Time Press, Santa Fe, 1985. First appeared in *Montemora.* **Lewis Turco,** "Leviathan," from A Maze of Monsters by Lewis Turco, Livingston University Press, 1986. First appeared under the title "Sounding," in *Escarpments,* 1985. **Constance Urdang,** "The Other Life," from Only the World by Constance Urdang, Pitt Poetry Series, University of Pittsburgh Press, 1983, first appeared in *Poetry,* copyright ©1983 by The Modern Poetry Association, and printed by permission of the editors of *Poetry* and of The University of Pittsburgh Press. **Ellen Bryant Voigt,** "Suicides," copyright ©1976 by Ellen Bryant Voigt, reprinted from Claiming Kin by permission of Wesleyan University Press. **Dorothy Ward,** "Whale" first appeared in *Amphora Review* and *Green Fuse.* **Margaret Weaver,** "Stranded Whales" first appeared in Finding the Name edited by Elisavietta Ritchie, copyright ©1983 by Wineberry Press. **Sarah Brown Weitzman,** "Whales to Oceanus," first appeared in *Grub Street* No. 10, 1980; reprinted in *Waterways,* Vol. 3, No. 6, August, 1982, and *Center for Environmental Education Report,* Vol. 3, No. 3, October, 1985. **Richard Wilbur,** "Advice to a Prophet" from Advice to a Prophet and Other Poems, copyright ©1959 by Richard Wilbur, reprinted by permission of Harcourt Brace Jovanovich, Inc. **Peter Wild,** "Seals," first appeared in *Arts 2.* **Adrienne Wolfert,** "Suicides," from Natal Fire by Adrienne Wolfert, Brandon Press, 1980, first appeared in *Poet Lore.*

Typeset by Heidi Glang of HG Editorial Services
Cover and book design by Mary Ann Briggs
Printed by Smith Lithograph Corporation, Rockville, MD